D1234609

The
Electronic
Library

The LexingtonBooks Special Series in Libraries and Librarianship

Richard D. Johnson, General Editor

The
Electronic
Library

The Impact of Automation
on Academic Libraries

Hugh F. Cline
Loraine T. Sinnott
Educational Testing Service

LexingtonBooks
D.C. Heath and Company
Lexington, Massachusetts
Toronto

Library of Congress Cataloging in Publication Data

Cline, Hugh F.
   The electronic library.

   Includes index.
   1. Libraries, University and college—United States—Automation—Case
studies.   2. Research libraries—United States—Automation—Case studies.
3. Library surveys—United States.   I. Sinnott, Loraine, T.   II. Title.
Z675.U5C624   1983   027.7'0973   81–47871
ISBN 0–669–05113–6

Copyright © 1983 by D.C. Heath and Company

Published simultaneously in Canada

Printed in the United States of America

International Standard Book Number: 0–669–05113–6

Library of Congress Catalog Card Number: 81–47871

To Pat and Warren

Contents

Figures and Tables

Preface

This book is a report of comparative case studies examining the effect of automation on the structure and functioning of university libraries. It draws upon theoretical perspectives derived from earlier studies of the impact of technology on complex organizations. Our research was supported by the U.S. Office of Education and Educational Testing Service.

The methods employed were primarily those of anthropological field work. Analyses have drawn upon data collected in visits to the libraries of the University of Chicago, Northwestern University, Stanford University, and the University of Washington. During forty-two days of field work, we divided the interviewing of 216 academic librarians and university administrators. These data have been supplemented by other information supplied in statistical summaries and reports prepared by each of the libraries.

This is the second book completed by the authors reporting on organizational analyses of academic libraries. The first examined collection-development policies and practices in the libraries of Earlham College, Stockton State College, Brown University, Pennsylvania State University, the University of North Carolina, the University of Wisconsin, and the University of California, Los Angeles.

The present project, as well as the former, has been organized to insure a dual return on the invested resources. First, it is intended that the book make a basic contribution to the social-scientific study of complex organizations. Second, the data collection and analyses have been structured to provide perspectives on policy issues that are of current concern to academic librarians. The search for such a dual payoff reflects the authors' commitment to policy-relevant social-science research.

We address this book to several audiences. First, we intend to demonstrate to social scientists that university libraries can add important and interesting dimensions to the understanding of structure and function in complex organizations. Second, we intend to demonstrate to university librarians what potentially fruitful insights may emerge from the social-scientific study of organizations. Third, we foresee the usefulness of this material to students enrolled in both library-science and social-science courses who are interested in comparative organizational studies. And finally, we direct our work to personnel involved in administrative activities in university libraries, in their host institutions, and in public and private funding agencies . . . all dedicated to promoting the long-range welfare of a distinguished cultural resource.

Acknowledgments

We wish to acknowledge the gracious assistance of the librarians and university administrators who provided the data upon which this book's analyses are based. Our expression of appreciation to the following library directors should be understood to include all their colleagues: Stanley McElderry, formerly librarian, the University of Chicago; John McGowan, university librarian, Northwestern University libraries; David Weber, university librarian, Stanford University; and Merle Boylan, director, the University of Washington library. Our gratitude is also extended to Lawrence Papier, Henry T. Drennan, and Adrienne Chute, of the Library Research and Demonstration Branch, Division of Library Programs, U.S. Department of Education. Duane E. Webster, director of the Office of Management Studies, Association of Research Libraries, provided invaluable aid in every phase of our design, execution, and dissemination activities.

We wish to record our indebtedness to our Educational Testing Service colleagues, William Turnbull, past president; Robert Solomon, executive vice-president; Winton Manning, past senior vice-president; Ernest Anastasio, vice-president for Research Management; and Garlie Forehand, research director, for providing the facilities and intellectual environment that so fruitfully support this type of research. In particular, the administrative support of Eugene Horkay, the editorial assistance of Elsa Rosenthal, and the administrative assistance of Lois Harris, Lois Barrett, and Joanne Farr are gratefully acknowledged.

1 Introduction

The discipline of sociology, which studies the development, organization, and function of human groups, provides the general theoretical perspective for the research reported in this book. Two of the major subfields within this discipline, the study of formal or complex organizations and the study of social change, provide the specific framework. Sociologists have offered several definitions of complex organizations, but three features appear essential to defining the nature of such groupings:

1. a collectivity of individuals who have reached some minimal agreement to cooperate in accomplishing common goals;
2. a structural differentiation of tasks and specific labor assignments among members; and,
3. a shared recognition of boundaries of the organization that delineates both members and nonmembers.[1]

The theoretical and empirical literature on complex organizations is vast and a plethora of different, yet complementary, perspectives has been employed in their study. For example, some studies focus on decision making and analyze organizational activities as evidence of rationality applied to maximize gains or profits. Others review patterns or styles in management and define their effect on organizational outcomes. Still others examine and characterize interpersonal communications among organizational members. Empirical studies have encompassed many different types of organizations, including labor unions, hospitals, schools, businesses, prisons, military units, and political parties.[2]

A parallel, pervasive, and continuing interest of sociology has been social change, and a challenging theoretical and speculative literature on the topic ranges from the theories of Talcott Parsons[3] to those of the futurists.[4] In recent decades, various sociologists have focused their interest in social change to study, specifically, how technology affects a society. Our investigation also follows that course.

Technology, as we broadly define it, includes any new knowledge introduced principally to improve goal attainment. Thus, topics under the rubric of technology's effect on complex organizations might include how a prison is changed by a new penal philosophy, how a school is altered because of a new mathematics curriculum, or how a bank is modified by the introduction of an electronic funds-transfer system. At issue is a new body of expert knowledge introduced into an organization and an expectation, among others, of improved efficiency or expanded services.

Because the expert knowledge is new to the organization, it is not uniformly shared by all members. This condition gives rise to situations in which supervisors may not command the same mastery of operations as do their supervisees. By virtue of such exclusive competencies, knowledgeable individuals frequently accrue influence and power that exceeds their formal position, duties, and responsibilities. This situation produces, then, a series of effects that cycle through the organization with varying degrees of amplitude. Communication patterns are frequently rearranged in fundamental ways, authority relationships may be modified, sources of satisfaction and morale may be altered, and new career paths may emerge.

For several decades now, university libraries have employed various types of computer-aided systems to accomplish a variety of bibliographic-processing activities. However, in recent years, the rate of adopting computer systems has escalated rapidly. Almost all university libraries are now employing some type of computer-aided system in their operations, and it appears certain that their commitment to automated support will expand even further. Hence, when we searched for organizational locations in which to examine the effect of technological innovation, university libraries emerged as most attractive sites. There are very few organizations in our society that are undergoing more fundamental transformation as a result of automation. The objective of this investigation was to observe, document, and analyze how university libraries are adopting and adapting to the new computer-aided systems as they attempt to accomplish their multiple and varying objectives.

University Libraries as Complex Organizations

The major goal of a university library is to acquire, document, and facilitate the use of information and materials that support the research and teaching programs of its host institution. The activities in which university libraries engage to achieve these objectives can be divided into the following categories:

1. collection management,
2. acquisitions,
3. cataloging,
4. circulation, and
5. reference services.

It should be pointed out that the tasks in these categories overlap substantially.

Collection management, frequently referred to as *collection development,* primarily encompasses those tasks that lead to the selection of materials for addition to the library. Many individuals contribute to the selection process, including library staff, faculty, students, administrators, and representatives of commercial vendors or jobbers of library materials. However, only a subset actually are authorized by the library to spend money for new acquisitions. The others funnel their suggestions to those formally designated as item selectors. Selectors rely on a variety of printed sources to help them identify new titles, including professional and trade journals, acquisition lists from other libraries, subject or geographical-area bibliographies, cataloging data from the Library of Congress, and publishers' announcements. In addition to selection, collection management encompasses the evaluation, placement, weeding, and preservation of holdings. Typically, however, item selection consumes most of the resources a library allocates to collection management.

The second major group of activities, *acquisitions,* includes the tasks associated with ordering materials, monitoring deliveries, and approving payments. The terms *collection management* and *acquisitions* are often used interchangeably, thus causing some confusion. In this book, we distinguish between the more intellectual and the more clerical aspects of materials acquisition, calling the former collection management and the latter acquisitions. The process of acquisitions can be broken down into the following eight steps:

1. searching library files to insure a title has not already been ordered or is not presently part of the collection,
2. collecting sufficient bibliographic information describing the item to allow specification of the order,
3. selecting the appropriate supplier,
4. preparing and dispatching an order,
5. monitoring delivery,
6. initiating claims or cancellations in the case of nondelivery,
7. checking items sent by suppliers against order forms and invoices, and
8. initiating the procedures for accounting and payment.

Academic libraries acquire material through the fulfillment of firm orders, through standing order or approval plans, through exchange agreements, and through gifts. *Firm orders* are book and serial selections initiated by library staff, faculty, or other library users. *Standing-order plans* are contractual agreements with suppliers of materials that result in the library's automatically being sent by the suppliers all publications of a given kind. For example, a jobber may be contracted to acquire for the library all new publications coming from U.S. university presses. The library is bound to buy everything the jobber sends. *Approval plans* are similar to standing orders but differ in that the library may return materials after reviewing them. *Exchange agreements* are arrangements with other institutions, primarily foreign academic institutions, to supply documents to which they have access in exchange for documents available to the library. Most exchange partners are within countries in which material is difficult to acquire through purchase. Bibliographic control may be poor, currency exchange difficult, or political unrest common. *Gifts* are received by academic libraries both through their own solicitation activities and through unsolicited donations. The library of an alumnus may be bequeathed; a faculty member may divert the titles publishers send for review; or a local citizen may decide to clean out a basement.

Books account for most of the new titles acquired by university libraries. However, libraries collect other formats, the most important of which is the *serial*. A serial is a publication issued in ordered parts, usually with no fixed date for termination. Typically, its parts are associated with a common title. Serials include regularly issued publications such as periodicals, newspapers, and annuals, and irregularly issued publications, including monographic series and sets. The money spent on purchasing serials in many university libraries exceeds that spent on buying books.

An increasing proportion of the university library's materials budget is being used to buy *microforms,* materials that have been photographically reduced in size. They are usually distributed in the form of negatives. Because of their relatively inexpensive duplication cost and their size, microforms allow libraries to obtain and maintain materials at costs substantially less than those involved in the acquisition of the original documents. Microforms can be grouped generally as follows: microfilm, microfiche, ultrafiche, microopaques, and aperture cards.

In addition to books, serials, and microforms, university libraries collect technical reports, government documents, musical scores, play and film scripts, manuscripts, slides, sound recordings, and ephemera; that is, pamphlets and materials clipped from newspapers, magazines, and other types of documents. Recently, numerical data files stored on magnetic tape have also become targets for acquisition.

Cataloging, the third group of activities, includes the tasks of recording, describing, and indexing the holdings of a library. Cataloging determines the number and kinds of access points for retrieving each item. The process of cataloging material has two components: description and subject analysis. *Descriptive cataloging* involves gathering data about the material as an object, without regard to what it is about. The title, author or editor, edition, publisher, and date of publication are part of the material's description. Other examples of attributes that qualify as descriptive data are physical size, the presence of an index or bibliography, the place of publication, and the number of pages, volumes, or illustrations. For translated works, the name of the translator is included in the descriptive data. For titles that are part of a series, bibliographic information about the series may be included with the material's description.

Subject analysis is concerned with the substantive content of the material. It involves selecting the topics that most appropriately describe a title's contents. Subject analysis also involves selecting from among appropriate subject classifications that which will be used as the basis for a code referred to as a *call number*. The code assigns the material a shelf location, determined by the location of similarly classified material. All catalog records representing the material also carry the call number. The Dewey Decimal and the Library of Congress (LC) classification systems are the basis for almost all coding schemes used by the libraries. Most school and public libraries rely on the Dewey system. Although some university libraries also rely on Dewey, most follow the LC scheme.

The data resulting from the descriptive-cataloging component of the cataloging process form the core of a catalog record. Most libraries place the data on three-by-five-inch cards, with one card usually providing enough space for the record of one title. The public catalog is the major repository for catalog records. Here several copies of a record are filed, varying only in their headings, also called *entries*. Among the different headings for a record are the topics established by the subject analysis, the title, and the party or parties responsible for authoring the material. Other ways in which a library user might seek or desire to find the material represented by the record may generate still more headings and, in turn, catalog cards for the public files. Cards are arranged in a dictionary like manner based on their headings. Sometimes author, title, and subject entry cards are identified. Sometimes discrete files are used for one or all of these card categories.

The most common use of the public catalog is to retrieve the call number for a particular work, for which the user knows the title or author, or at least has partial information about one of these attributes. In addition to helping users locate particular works, public catalogs support more general explorations of the library's holdings. A user, for example, may wish to know what the library has on a particular subject or by a given author. Public catalogs group cards by subject and author to facilitate the retrieval of such information.

A catalog loses its effectiveness as a tool for locating material if catalogers vary the entries they employ for authors, titles, and subjects and do not make appropriate cross references. To help them formulate entries that match previously used headings and determine all the cross references that should be attached to an entry, catalogers depend on lists and files that document the practices of their library. In fact, the maintenance of these constantly changing stores of data is a major cataloging activity. The information in the lists and files provide what is referred to as the public catalog's *authority structure.*

Cataloging material is time-consuming. For example, the Library of Congress estimates that its catalogers need three to five hours to catalog the typical book.[5] To ease some of the burden of cataloging, libraries share the records they create. The first library to make its cataloging data widely available was LC. At the turn of the century, it began selling copies of its catalog cards. Ever since, LC has played a dominant role in providing catalog records to libraries, even though records from other libraries are now also widely disseminated. Its supremacy is due to the fact that the LC catalogs far more than any other single institution—acquiring in one year what many university libraries have taken their lifetimes to collect.

If the data in borrowed catalog records must often be revised, added to, or reorganized, the gains in sharing data diminish. Two factors increase the likelihood that a cataloging record created by one institution will match that created by another. First, librarians have established cataloging standards. Second, librarians use common sources to guide their selection of record entries.

In 1908, shortly after LC began its card service, the nation's libraries, through the American Library Association, adopted a formal set of rules for descriptive cataloging, rules that have since undergone a number of revisions. They are now referred to as the Anglo-American Cataloging Rules (AACR). Cataloging was guided by rules before 1908 but not by a uniform code. The action of the American Library Association resulted in standards to which all libraries could refer for guidance in devising their own procedures. In principle, librarians accept their profession's standards. In practice, libraries vary in their adherence to the rules. School and community libraries, for example, follow the rules much less rigidly than do university libraries, which tend toward more complete compliance.

The cataloging rules set forth the types of information that should be included in records, how it should be described and presented, and the general layout of the information. Despite their meticulousness, the rules do not completely determine what a record will look like. Cataloging requires numerous judgments. The records created by two catalogers, both of whom follow the rules to the letter, will not necessarily be the same. Perhaps most important among the judgments are the topics chosen as subject entries, the titles chosen to represent works that have appeared in many editions, and the forms selected for authors' names—all elements of what was earlier referred to as a catalog's authority structure.

The Anglo-American Cataloging Rules do not include a subject thesaurus to guide subject selections. Indeed they do not cover subject cataloging at all. The rules do not set forth preferred name and title entries. Although they offer extensive guidance in determining forms for titles and authors, the application of these principles does not always lead to the same conclusion.

The heterogeneity in types of collections libraries house, as well as the needs they address, makes it difficult to develop a list of entries suitable to all libraries. Furthermore it would be virtually impossible for the issuers of such a list to keep abreast of the required entries. As extensive as the collections of LC are, for example, the author of every other book it receives is new to the catalog.[6] Despite their shortcomings, just a handful of lists do in fact guide the entry selections of most libraries. Furthermore, libraries of the same type—for example, public, medical, academic—tend to use the same sources for guidance. University libraries, for example, rely heavily on lists distributed by LC.

The Library of Congress publishes the subject and name headings it uses for its own catalog records. Deferring to its choices eases the task of integrating catalog records obtained from the LC with locally prepared records. Indeed deferring to LC entry choices eases the job of integrating borrowed records in general because LC is the single most influential force in shaping the cataloging practices of the library community.

Before we leave our discussion of cataloging, it should be noted that differences in practice still abound even though most university libraries follow LC, some almost religiously. A library often catalogs titles for which LC has not yet issued and may never issue catalog data. Thus, many records are created with no external model to provide a standard. Differences also stem from local needs, entries used by LC that other libraries consider out-of-date, and local practices that would be costly to modify to conform to LC practice. The use of tools other than those published by LC also contributes to variations in practice. The National Library of Medicine, for instance, disseminates its subject headings, which are widely used by catalogers of medical collections.

Affiliated with cataloging materials are a series of clerical steps, often referred to as *end processing,* in which titles are prepared for shelving and circulation. Call numbers are mounted on the spines of volumes and selected bibliographic information entered within. Pockets for circulation cards and, if used, special devices for security against theft are also inserted.

After end processing, materials are placed on shelves, making them accessible to library users. An item's place in the collection is determined by the location of materials already in the collection. However, it is unlikely that the initially assigned shelf space will remain fixed. In fact, library holdings are constantly in motion. Items are taken from their shelves for use inside or outside the library. As the collection grows, volumes are moved to new shelves or are shifted right or left to accommodate new acquisitions.

Entire sections of the collection may be relocated in response to a reorganization of holdings. Reclassification may send items to new areas of the library, such as a branch, another floor, or a remote storage facility.

Circulation involves those activities concerned with the movement of library holdings. The activities can be divided into two groups: tasks associated with maintaining the integrity of the shelf areas and tasks associated with managing the formal, but temporary, removal of material from their shelf locations, including the setting and enforcing of rules by which users have access to the collections. Included within the former group of tasks are:

1. shelving new acquisitions,
2. reshelving materials,
3. withdrawing items from holdings,
4. "reading" shelves to locate misshelved items,
5. searching for items users cannot locate,
6. carrying out collection reorganizations, and
7. carrying out inventories of holdings.

In addition to being checked out to library users, material may be formally, but temporarily, removed from holdings for interlibrary loan, binding or mending, or to become part of a reserve collection. Current information on the status of removed items is maintained and monitored so that material held by users beyond the stipulated borrowing period can be identified, items that are missing can be distinguished from those that have been formally removed, and material held by one user and requested by another can be recalled.

Most circulation systems centralize information on the location of titles in an *exception file;* that is, a file in which an entry is made whenever an item that is part of the circulating collection is unavailable for lending. If the exception file does not contain an entry for an item, it is assumed to be in its proper location on the shelf. Unfortunately, this assumption is often unwarranted. Misshelved items and lost items that have not yet come to the attention of the library are common in university libraries.

Circulation activities make it possible for library users to borrow library materials. Of course, users must first identify the material they need. Among library activities, the most essential are those that directly facilitate the user-library interaction. These activities are part of *reference services.* In particular, reference services include:

1. helping users locate and retrieve needed material, searching and borrowing from the holdings of other libraries, if necessary;
2. conducting formal or informal instructional sessions on library use or the use of particular library tools, on an individual or group basis;

3. compiling bibliographies or collecting data in response to user questions or requests; and
4. contracting for and managing the access to commercially distributed bibliographic data bases.

Logically, the last activity could have been subsumed within collection development. However, most libraries do not acquire machine-readable bibliographic data bases. Rather, they purchase access to them through telecommunication networks. Thus, they acquire a service rather than an object. Libraries usually distinguish between the two, separating their budget for search services from their budget for material acquisitions.

Numerous tools facilitate reference activities. Primary among them are guides that classify—by subject, author, or some other manner—collections of documents; for example, books, technical reports, or articles in periodicals. Bibliographies, indexes, and card and book catalogs are included in this group. Of equal importance are tools that indicate which libraries hold given documents or what the holdings of a particular library are. A compilation of the holdings of more than one library is referred to as a *union catalog*. Numerous partial or complete lists of the book or serial holdings of libraries exist in formats that promote dissemination, such as books or microfiche. Tools facilitating the location of technical reports, conference proceedings, and other types of so-called fugitive literature are not as prevalent.

Having reviewed the major activities of a university library, we now turn to a brief description of how these activities are structured organizationally. Figure 1-1 is a highly simplified organizational chart for a hypothetical university library. Nevertheless, a number of observations can be made. An obvious but crucial aspect of a university library derives from the fact that it is an operating unit within a larger organization, the host university. Resources are made available by the university administration to the library director, who in turn is accountable to the administration. The library director frequently enlists the assistance of an advisory committee to help oversee library operations. The members of the committee are typically faculty who are interested in library policy. Frequently students and the university administration are also represented on the committee. Because the committee operates in an advisory capacity, a dotted line connects the library director and committee block in figure 1-1. Library directors usually have administrative and personnel units to assist in the management of library operations. These units frequently operate in a staff capacity to the director and rarely exercise direct supervisory authority over operations.

Technical services include those processing activities that precede the placement of new materials on library shelves. In general, the technical-services division of a library is responsible for setting in motion the actions of publishers, jobbers, and other suppliers that lead to their sending

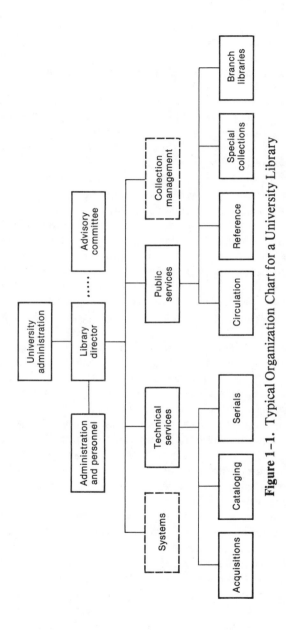

Figure 1-1. Typical Organization Chart for a University Library

material to the library. The division is also responsible for monitoring the activities of suppliers, receiving the material, and preparing it for shelving. The standard components of a technical-services division are the acquisitions and cataloging departments. In figure 1-1, we have suggested a third unit—serials. Often the acquisition and cataloging of serials is separated organizationally from the processing of monographs.

Public services contain those units that link users to the information or materials they seek. A standard unit within public services is a reference department. The library's circulation department may be within public services, but its location is far less predictable than reference. Many circulation tasks are classified appropriately as part of technical services, justifying alternate organizational arrangements. Some libraries place circulation within technical services; some allow it to reside independently without attachment to either technical or public services.

Branch or departmental libraries often are part of public services, even though branches are responsible for performing a number of acquisitions and cataloging tasks. The reference and circulation departments noted in figure 1-1 refer to units within the central library. Branches usually maintain their own reference and circulation units.

Most university libraries maintain a separate department for special collections, frequently locating it within public services. A special collection is a gathering of materials for a particular research activity. The materials may be of a certain format, on a certain subject, or from a certain historical period or geographical area. The materials are collected and organized to facilitate advanced research activities on a highly specialized topic; for example, ethnic religions or the history of the U.S. Southwest. As with branches, special-collection units tend to handle their own reference and circulation activities.

The responsibility for selecting new acquisitions is shared by a number of individuals. For most selectors, collection development is only a part-time concern. This group includes faculty and librarians in reference and branch units. Bibliographers are usually the only selectors devoting essentially all their time to collection development. Bibliographers are library employees with expertise in the identification, selection, and acquisition of scholarly material. They limit their efforts to specific substantive or geographic areas, such as history of science or Slavic studies. Although bibliographers are often responsible for systemwide coordination of collection development, the holdings of the central library are the main focus of their activity. Branch, reference, and special-collection units usually build their collections with little assistance from bibliographers.

The organizational location of collection management varies widely among university libraries. Sometimes it is situated in public services; sometimes it is a separate unit reporting to the director; and frequently item selectors are distributed in different departments throughout the library. Because of the variation in the organization of this function, the collection-management block in figure 1–1 is circumscribed with broken lines.

Automation activities in university libraries may be under the direction of a systems unit, the final element in figure 1–1. Both the organizational location and function of systems units vary widely among libraries depending upon the nature and extent of automated activities. For this reason, the systems block in the figure also appears with broken lines.

It is also possible to identify several different organizational patterns of systems personnel in university libraries. One pattern occurs in a library that employs a single computer-based system to support many facets of its operations. Members of the systems department are responsible for designing, implementing, and maintaining the various components of automation, which are intended eventually to be inclusive of most library operations. In such a library, a separate systems department exists and usually reports to the library director, reflecting the fact that the department's scope is the entire library.

A second organizational pattern occurs in university libraries in which various functions have been or are in the process of being automated in an independent fashion. For example, a library may decide to automate its circulation operations by purchasing a system from an outside vendor. Such a circulation system will be self-contained and will not directly influence activities in other units of the library. In this instance, systems personnel might report to the head of circulation. The scope of responsibility and level of activity of these individuals are focused on the area in which automation is underway or in place. Consequently, their influence is less pervasive than in the first pattern discussed above.

A third type of organizational pattern for systems personnel occurs in the library where responsibility for designing, implementing, and enhancing automated library activities is given to a group outside the library; for example, the staff of the university computing center. One or more individuals from different units throughout the library may be given responsibility for liaison with the computer-center personnel. In this instance, the influence that frequently accrues to those associated with fundamental organizational change is allocated primarily to outsiders, persons not formally under the supervision or control of the library. The organizational location and functioning of systems personnel will be a major object of inquiry throughout this book.

Automation and Libraries

As may be inferred from our description of library activities, the operation of a university library is driven by data—its creation and storage, retrieval and review, modification and manipulation. Indeed librarians spend considerably more time processing information about books and serials than they devote to handling the objects themselves. Computers are amply suited to supporting data-processing activities. It was inevitable that librarians eventually would examine the possibility of their use within libraries.

Widespread interest in computer applications evolved during the 1960s. Over the decade, university libraries experienced unprecedented growth in the demand for their services and in the rate of their acquisitions, directly benefiting from the phenomenal growth in the enrollments and budgets of their host institutions. The increasing workloads in processing and circulation brought many manual systems to the limits of their effectiveness—and often beyond. For example, insurmountable backlogs of uncataloged material began to accumulate in many libraries. Indeed in some of these institutions, unprocessed titles acquired during this period still line shelves in storage areas. In response to their new levels of activity, libraries hired more staff. However, as the decade progressed, another kind of solution to what were primarily data-processing problems became feasible—computers.

At a time in which the number of extant computers exceeds the world's population[7] and computers are routinely used for tasks as complicated as guiding spaceships to far-off planets, it is easy to lose sight of how recent is the technological achievement of the computer. Although the first computer was built just before World War II, general-purpose computers were not widely available until the 1960s; and applications approaching the complexity of those desired by libraries were not commonplace until the end of the decade. Thus it was not until the 1960s that computers realistically could be considered by libraries as tools to support their processing activities.

However, need and feasibility were not the only factors converging to spark widespread interest among librarians in computer-based library systems. The increasing visibility of computers to the community of university librarians was another influential factor. Throughout the decade university after university acquired computers to support research, instructional programs, and administrative data processing. Because of their ties to so many other parts of the university, campus computer centers rapidly became centers of activity and attention. At the same time, several highly visible conferences and studies trumpeted the benefits and the feasibility of using computers in libraries.[8]

Numerous automation projects were initiated during the 1960s. Stephen Salmon provides an excellent overview of the types of projects libraries undertook.[9] Most of the systems that emerged before the end of the decade were batch-oriented, because, with few exceptions, universities did not develop or acquire timesharing systems until the late 1960s. Also, libraries initially concentrated on systems that would ease the burden of their operation, focusing on support for the so-called housekeeping functions of acquisitions, cataloging, and circulation. Widespread interest in systems that could aid the activities of the reference librarian or the library user did not emerge until the latter half of the 1970s. Most university librarians have begun only recently to explore the development of computer systems to support new types of information services. Innovations in information science have not been sparked by university libraries. Rather, they are due to projects like Information Transfer Experiments (INTREX)[10] and the Stanford Physics Information Retrieval System (SPIRES)[11] and to the commercial sector; for example, the work of Lockheed Information Systems and System Development Corporation in the area of on-line data retrieval.

For libraries, then, the 1960s were primarily years of system development and experimentation. By the 1970s initial optimism had given way to an awareness of the limitations of computer systems and wariness about their cost. Libraries continued cautiously to automate their operations though a decline in funding slowed their progress even more. Finding support for local development efforts was more difficult in the 1970s. The decade was one of retrenchment for colleges and universities, and money for nonessential projects was limited. Federal and private funding agencies turned from their earlier support of local development projects to favor projects that would aid the library community more generally.

Despite the slowing of progress, numerous computer-based library systems and services were introduced and marketed, most resulting from projects initiated in the previous decade. The commercial sector was the major contributor. Through the 1960s, it had sold libraries its hardware and its expertise. However, in the 1970s it went a step further. It packaged complete systems that libraries could readily install and use immediately. Most of these systems supported circulation. Because of the minimal preparation required before they can be used, the packages are dubbed *turnkey systems*.

The commercial sector also marketed computer-based services. Perhaps the best known of these systems is the on-line search service, which allows a library to explore data bases held in a remote computer facility through telecommunications networks like Tymnet and Telenet. The major commercial vendors of on-line search services are Lockheed Information Systems, now offering over one hundred data bases, System Development Corporation (SDC), now offering sixty data bases, and Bibliographic Retrieval Services (BRS), now offering about thirty data bases.

Libraries also contributed to the marketplace of systems and services that was born in the 1970s. Among the most significant of their contributions is the computer-based bibliographic-data cooperative, which gives its members access to a large pool of machine-readable catalog data. The pool contains records that have been contributed by coop members as well as the records of major data suppliers like LC. As with on-line search services, communication with the central computer facility housing the data base is made possible through the use of telecommunication systems. Coop members can order catalog cards based on the on-line records. In fact, they generally depend on the cooperative to supply cards of records they contribute to the data base as well as cards of records that have been created by other libraries.

The success of cooperatives is owed primarily to LC, and in particular to project MARC (Machine-Readable Cataloging). The objective of this LC project, which began in the mid 1960s, was to define a format for machine-readable catalog records. First, a format for books was established and later formats for films, manuscripts, maps, music, and serials were issued.

In 1969, the Library of Congress used the book format to disseminate in machine-readable form magnetic tapes of all of its cataloging of works in the English language. At present, LC's MARC tapes include books in all roman-alphabet languages and romanized records of books in Greek, Cyrillic, and south Asian languages. In 1982, LC's machine-readable book file surpassed 1.5-million entries. The Library of Congress also disseminates its cataloging of films, maps, and serials in machine-readable form. The serials file, the largest of the three, had 130,000 titles in 1982.[12]

Thus, the MARC project has resulted in a tremendous and continually growing pool of machine-searchable catalog records, the lifeline of the bibliographic-data cooperative. It also offered the library community the best candidate for a communication format that could be adopted by libraries preparing machine-readable records—the format employed by LC. The implications of this aspect of project MARC were not lost on the Ohio College Library Center, now called OCLC, Inc. In 1971, OCLC implemented the first computer-based bibliographic-data cooperative, using the MARC format for interlibrary communication.

The on-line system initially served some 50 libraries in the state of Ohio. By 1975, OCLC services were available to libraries in other states and OCLC membership stood at 700. At present, its membership is 3,000 libraries, growing at a rate of 15 percent a year.[13] To deliver its services to libraries, OCLC works primarily through regional organizations. Only about a dozen members deal directly with OCLC.

OCLC's data base contained 8.3-million records in 1982 and was increasing in size by more than a million records a year. A record submitted by an OCLC member joins the on-line data if no other record representing the work is part of the base. MARC records, though, supersede records contributed by OCLC members. Theoretically, then, no work can be represented by more than one catalog record. In reality, though, this is not the case. For example, 7 to 9 percent of the monographic records are estimated to be duplicates.[14] Reasons for duplication are many. For instance, a title may be labeled a serial by one library and a book by another. In such a case, the system assumes the records represent different works.

Initially MARC records from LC accounted for most of the data flowing into the OCLC system, but as OCLC's membership grew, the balance shifted in favor of member contributions. In 1974, for example, members contributed five times more records than did the LC through MARC.[15] Today MARC records account for less than 20 percent of the entire OCLC data base. However, the MARC data significantly surpass member contributions in their usefulness for cataloging. In 1979, it was found that the typical MARC record had been used twenty-nine times by OCLC members. The typical member-contributed record had been used four times. Only about 20 percent of the MARC records had never been used by a member library for cataloging. In contrast, nearly half of the member-contributed records had never been used.[16]

The United States has one other bibliographic-data cooperative with nationwide membership, the Research Libraries Information Network (RLIN), operated by the Research Libraries Group. RLIN is based on a system called BALLOTS (Bibliographic Automation of Large Library Operations using a Timesharing System), which in the mid-1970s was a bibliographic-data cooperative based at Stanford University and serving primarily libraries in California. A brief history of BALLOTS and RLIN will be given in chapter 2.

Membership in the Research Libraries Group (RLG) is open to members of the Association of Research Libraries, an organization for both university and non-university-affiliated research libraries.[17] One-hundred-and-ten libraries belong to the association. RLG membership is presently twenty-six libraries, up from four libraries in 1978, when RLIN was inaugurated. RLG also has one associate member and a dozen special members. The special members administer special collections like law and art. They include private, not-for-profit institutions such as museums and libraries within universities that have not joined RLG.

In addition to member and special-member libraries of the Research Libraries Group, 295 other libraries participate in the Research Libraries Information Network. Approximately one-third were BALLOTS users prior to its acquisition by RLG. Nearly three-fourths of the non-RLG participants in RLIN limit their use of the system to searching its files. They neither enter bibliographic data nor request catalog cards. The remaining 80 or so libraries enter records into the RLIN data base and order catalog cards. Most of these 80 libraries are members of the California Library Authority for Systems and Services (CLASS), a regional organization that acts as a broker for RLIN.

In 1982 the RLIN data base had 7.2-million records, representing approximately 5.3-million titles. Because the RLG membership has been expanding so rapidly over the past few years, no meaningful growth rate can at present be attached to the data base. In contrast to the OCLC system, a library has direct access to its local records, which are linked to records representing the same bibliographic entity. The *clustered-record design* allows each library to locate its own record but still provides the searcher with a single record showing all libraries that have indicated their holding of the title.

A third major computer-based bibliographic-data cooperative operates in the United States. It is called the Washington Library Network (WLN). Unlike OCLC and RLIN, WLN is regional in scope, serving the libraries of the Northwest. More than half of its eighty-five members reside in the state of Washington.[18] Other states with member libraries include Alaska, Idaho, Montana, and Oregon. One library from Arizona belongs to WLN, but WLN does not formally include the Arizona libraries in its range of membership. WLN is negotiating with libraries in California and British Columbia concerning their membership in WLN.

The Washington Library Network began its on-line bibliographic-data cooperative in 1977. Initially the system served only Washington state libraries, but by 1978 WLN was actively seeking out-of-state members. Its data base is presently 2.3-million records, growing at a rate of 8.25 percent a year. There are essentially no duplicate records in the data base.

Despite the similarity in their services, some fundamental differences distinguish OCLC, RLIN, and WLN.[19] Firstly, both WLN and RLIN maintain all records contributed by members on-line. As was mentioned earlier, OCLC maintains only that record contributed first. As a result, in addition to providing catalog-data-resource files, WLN and RLIN also provide catalog-maintenance facilities. Second, OCLC's data base is perceived by many librarians to contain a higher percentage of substandard cataloging than is contained in the data base of WLN and RLIN. Because it has desired to interfere as little as possible with the procedures of its users, OCLC has imposed few cataloging standards on its users. In contrast, before a record contributed by a member enters the WLN data base, it is reviewed and edited by a central body responsible for quality control. RLIN's approach to quality control has elements of both OCLC and WLN policy. RLIN does not force standards on its users. However, an attractive financial incentive is maintained to encourage adherence to standards.

Finally, the cooperatives differ in the ease with which their files can be searched for records that are only generically defined. Examples of generically defined sets of records include entries representing works on a given subject or by a given author. For the technical-service librarian, browsability is not typically an essential feature of a system. He or she usually searches the data base of a cooperative for a precisely defined record. The title and author of the work are known or the librarian is armed with an identification code, such as a LC card number, a unique number assigned to each record LC creates. Public-service librarians and library users, on the other hand, often need to uncover all that is available concerning some generally defined information need. For them, browsability is a critical feature.

Compared to WLN and RLIN, OCLC has relatively little browsing capacity. Entry is by way of identification codes that uniquely identify records—or by what are called *search keys*. A search key is a series of letters algorithmically derived from a work's title and author. In contrast, both RLIN and WLN provide considerably enhanced versions of the browsing possible with card catalogs. Among the enhancements are the capacity to combine entries logically and to search for isolated words in an entry. OCLC's more limited browsability makes the bibliographic-data cooperative less useful as a public-service tool than WLN or RLIN.

The three cooperatives market other services in addition to cataloging support. All now have systems that aid the acquisitions process. The data bases of the cooperatives are invaluable as aids in locating material for interlibrary loans. Their on-line records include identification symbols that note the libraries that have directly or indirectly through record use indicated ownership of a title. OCLC and RLIN maintain message-transfer systems to further facilitate interlibrary loans among their membership. OCLC has implemented a serials check-in system to help its members monitor the delivery of their subscriptions and a union-list system to help groups of libraries build national, regional, and local serials union lists.

There is considerable overlap in the libraries the cooperatives attempt to attract to their membership. This overlap is most pronounced with OCLC and WLN, both of whom encourage libraries of all types and sizes to join their organizations. Thus essentially all the libraries of the Northwest are candidates for membership in both OCLC and WLN. Libraries, however, are discouraged from joining more than one cooperative, by both the costs of multiple membership and the cooperatives themselves. Because their fees depend on volume of activity, all the cooperatives strive for the full participation of their members. In fact, libraries joining OCLC and WLN until recently had to agree to enter all their current cataloging into the cooperative's data base. In 1982, OCLC introduced a category of membership that did not carry this obligation.[20]

For each of the cooperatives, research libraries are a particularly important market. For RLG, in fact, they are the only target group. Although RLIN is marketed through CLASS to libraries of all types, RLG's primary objective is to serve the nation's research libraries by providing a communications system to support a number of programs, the most important of which thus far has been the sharing of bibliographic data. However, even for OCLC, research-library membership is essential. Although they account for less than 5 percent of OCLC's membership, research libraries, along with LC, account for 60 percent of the original cataloging entering the

OCLC data base.[21] In fact, the loss of some of its research libraries to RLG has contributed to OCLC price increases.[22]

Bibliographic-data cooperatives have become an essential part of the library community. However, fundamental changes in their structure and function are most likely. Critical issues requiring resolution include their interrelationship, the optimal hardware and software configuration of a cooperative, and the library activities that can best be served by systems maintained by cooperatives. In the 1980s, libraries will busy themselves transferring systems developed by one library or group of libraries to another environment. Commercial concerns will busy themselves developing and marketing enhancements to their turnkey systems. However, because cooperatives affect so many libraries, discussion and action relating to the future of bibliographic cooperatives are likely to engage most of the attention of the community throughout the decade.

Research Methodology

This book is based on a series of four case studies conducted in the spring and summer of 1979. However the observations it offers have been considerably enriched by a commitment to the study of academic libraries that began in 1977 and has resulted in, among other things, interviews with some five hundred academic librarians and the in-depth analysis of a dozen libraries, all but one with multiunit organizations.

The 1979 case studies focused on automation and its effects on the structure and operation of university libraries. The institutions selected for study were the libraries of the University of Chicago, Northwestern University, Stanford University, and the University of Washington. A number of criteria were applied in the selection of these sites. The libraries of Chicago, Northwestern, and Stanford were outstanding candidates for study primarily because each had been involved in the implementation of sophisticated computer-based library systems, and each had extensive experience with the operation of such systems. The latter was a particularly important criterion, making more probable that long-term rather than short-term, and possibly transient, effects would be observed. The University of Washington was outstanding as a candidate for inclusion in the study primarily because it was just beginning what was planned to be an extensive commitment to automated systems. It thus presented a sharp contrast to the other members of the group.

Because the use of computer systems is so pervasive among university libraries, identifying a major research library just beginning the path to automation is considerably more difficult than identifying major research libraries with extensive experience. In fact more libraries emerged as appropriate candidates for inclusion in the study based on their extensive experience than we were able to select. Budget constraints limited the total number of sites to four. Unfortunately the many perspectives offered by the larger group of candidates could not all be captured by any subset of four. In the next chapter we will describe in detail each of the selected sites and discuss the dimensions in which they provided interesting points of comparison.

Our major data-collection techniques during the field work were interviews, observation of computer-supported activities, and the collection of documents such as annual reports, statistical summaries, and papers about the computer systems at the sites. About fifty-five librarians were interviewed at each site. Although the majority of interviewees were middle managers, almost all areas and levels of the organization were represented in the group selected.

A variety of topics was covered with considerable overlap from interview to interview, both within a library and across the four sites. During an interview we pursued from a number of perspectives how the library's computer-based systems had affected the interviewee, either directly or indirectly. An example of an interview schedule for the head of a technical-services unit is given in table 1-1. Such lists of interview topics provided structure for the interviews but by design also allowed considerable flexibility to accommodate additional topics. Although we were sensitive to the problem of "getting off the track," we generally encouraged interviewees to

Table 1-1
Sample Interview Schedule—Automation Impact Study

Interview Schedule for Assistant Director, Technical Services

---

1. Overall organization and operation of technical services.

2. History of automation projects.

3. Plans for future automation activities.

4. The different ways in which you personally might use the _____ system.

5. Your impression of how the _____ system has affected or possibly changed the manner in which you perform your job.

6. Your communication patterns with others: both formal; for example, meetings you regularly attend, reporting structure; and informal; for example, those you may contact to solve work-related problems.

7. The effects of the _____ system on interactions between branch libraries and the main library.

8. The present and future effects of automation on both collection development and collection use.

9. The ways in which experience with automated systems may influence a librarian's future career.

---

pursue other points if they were at all relevant to the effect of automation on the structure and functioning of the library. Indeed as the field work continued, many of these unanticipated issues became important subtopics for later interviews.

We took notes to document the sessions. Tape recorders were not used. Subsequently we dictated reconstructed versions of those parts of sessions considered particularly informative or critical. This format allowed us to share more easily the most crucial interview data.

The field work included two visits to each library. The first was considerably shorter than the second, lasting only two days. The second required about ten days. The purpose of the preliminary visits was twofold. First we wanted to introduce ourselves and the study to each library director and the senior staff. This objective was accomplished in a joint meeting, which included a formal presentation of the study plans. Second, we wanted to learn enough about each site to plan our subsequent field-work activities. This end was accomplished primarily through a series of hour-long interviews with key staff members, most of whom were senior administrators. The interviewees were asked to:

1. describe the structure and operation of the area they supervised,
2. describe the use of computers within this area, and
3. name individuals they considered good informants about the structure and operation of particular departments.

Shortly after a preliminary visit, we prepared a detailed schedule of interviews and observation periods and mailed the schedule to the library director. The schedule named each staff member we wished to talk to and suggested a date and time. In selecting the interviewees, we relied extensively on the recommendations gathered during the preliminary visit. The schedule included an interview with at least one university administrator. This individual had been recommended to us by the library director as that university administrator concerned with overall fiscal planning for the university and with particular responsibility for the library budget.

The topics to be discussed with each interviewee were enclosed with the interview schedule, allowing the library director to see in explicit terms what the interviews would involve. The director was asked to forward each list of topics to the appropriate interviewee, thus permitting the interviewee also to find out what issues would be addressed during an interview.

We thought it essential that all library-staff members, whether on the interview schedule or not, learn about the study prior to the field-work activities. The library directors cooperated fully, agreeing to publish a summary of the investigation in their library newsletters and enclosing with each list of interview topics a memorandum describing the study. In addition, at the beginning of each visit we held a seminar, open to the library staff, in which we discussed our prior research in libraries and summarized the study in which their library was participating. Through these efforts, numerous problems encountered in organizational casework were avoided. We were not perceived as agents of the administration or as evaluators who had come to assess staff performance. Also library staff had a framework within which to place our contacts with them; thus with just a few introductory remarks, interviews or observations could begin within an appropriate context.

Data analysis required reviewing and digesting an enormous amount of information. One of our first tasks was to synthesize the data into detailed descriptive accounts of the sites. We also culled the data for patterns, putting together what was said by one interviewee with what was said by another and adding relevant information from documents and our observations. During our review of the data sources, a number of theoretical and policy issues emerged. After their formal identification, we returned to the data sources to conduct a more systematic search for information pertaining to those issues.

The reliability of data collected by observations and interviews must be called into question. Investigators may select atypical moments to make their observations. Individuals may behave in an unusual manner under the eye of an observer. An interviewee may misstate facts, present rumor as truth, repeat misinformation. What parts of events are recalled and how they are remembered vary from individual to individual. Compounding all reliability problems is the individual field worker, through whom data must filter before they are incorporated into field notes.

We could not counter all the forces undermining the accuracy of our data. However, we did build into our procedures a number of ways to increase reliability. The same question was answered by numerous individuals, representing various levels of the organization and various departments. Furthermore, the repetition of questions carried across libraries. We scheduled observation periods over several days and at different times during the day. We employed a number of strategies to make staff comfortable with our presence, both during interviews and during observation periods. As we analyzed and synthesized our data, we attempted to verify information by cross-checking data derived from different sources, depending on documents collected during our work as well as our notes from interviews and observations.

Another shortcoming of the case-study methodology is its limited generalizability. We examined only four institutions. The extent to which conclusions derived from our work have general applicability must be questioned. We are confident, though, that the statements we make in the following chapters will provide a point of comparison of value to others when examining their own experience. Indeed, it is our hope that this book will stimulate the so often rewarding exercise of self-examination.

Our work was an exploratory undertaking. We did not begin with hypotheses to test. Rather, we wished to discover, with no preconceived ideas, how libraries have been affected by automation. It is also our hope that the findings we report will stimulate more focused questions for future research.

Organization of the Book

In the final pages of this introductory chapter, we provide a brief preview of the remaining chapters of the book. Chapter 2 is a rather detailed description of each of the four case-study libraries. It also includes several comparisons of the libraries that are relevant to subsequent discussions. The descriptions are historical, for they portray the development of automation activities. However, the descriptions are also analytic, for they examine how each library is organized to accomplish the major functions common to all university libraries.

Chapters 3 through 6 use an organizational perspective within which we present the results of our data collection and analyses. This perspective is adapted from an article prepared by G.C. Nielen[23] in which he describes a general framework useful for analyzing organizations. We have modified Nielen's structure to fit more appropriately the exploration of the impact of automation on the structure and operation of university libraries. The perspective includes four dimensions that correspond to chapters 3 through 6: structure, information, fiscal, and personnel.

Chapter 3 describes the structure dimension, which focuses upon task assignments and operating units in organizations. Here we identify the major tasks assigned to library units. We investigate how various units within the organization interact and the specific content of the stimuli and responses that characterize these relationships. We also discuss how automated activities have affected the accomplishment of collection management, acquisitiions, cataloging, circulation, and reference services. Our discussion takes account of the different loci of automation in university libraries: locally developed systems, commercial systems and services, and bibliographic cooperatives.

Chapter 4 takes up the information dimension. All organizations, including university libraries, distribute responsibility for decision making among their members and then design, implement, and monitor channels of communication to insure that decision makers have access to all relevant information. In examining this dimension, we locate key decision makers, map the data channels interconnecting them, and "listen" to a sample of the communication links. This chapter first presents a sociometric analysis of communication patterns in the libraries. It then focuses on technical and public services, raising the issue of the emerging eradication of this distinction in university libraries. The chapter also discusses communication with external organizations and concludes with a discussion of a new organizational format that may be emerging in university libraries.

Chapter 5 takes up the fiscal dimension of organizations. The focus of this chapter is on the policies and procedures by which resources are allocated to automation activities in libraries. The discussion reviews funding sources, the costs and benefits of automation, the constraints of physical plant, and the procedures for expanding and enhancing automated systems.

Chapter 6 takes up the fourth and final dimension of organizational analysis employed in this study, the personnel dimension. It reviews a series of personnel-related topics, including leadership style, personnel management, librarian-user interaction, and changing requirements for professional training.

We are acutely aware that these four dimensions are not exhaustive of all the aspects of university libraries that may be relevant to examining the effect of automation. We also recognize that these dimensions are highly interdependent and, therefore, are not mutually exclusive. Nevertheless, they do provide a convenient framework within which to classify and analyze the enormous amount of data collected in the course of this investigation. The final chapter of the book raises a number of policy issues related to automation in academic libraries.

Notes

1. For our earlier discussion of this point, see Hugh F. Cline and Loraine T. Sinnott, *Building Library Collections.*

2. Although it is now over fifteen years old, one of the best overviews of this field is still James G. March, ed., *Handbook of Organizations.*

3. Talcott Parsons, *Structure and Process in Modern Societies.*

4. See, for example, Alvin Toffler, *Future Shock;* see also his newer *The Third Wave.*

5. C.A. Goodwin, *The Library of Congress,* p. 90.

6. Ibid., p. 8.

7. R.A. Shaffer, "Computing Industry Is Finding That It's Vulnerable to Slump," *Wall Street Journal,* 16 April 1982, p. 35.

8. For example, see Gerald W. King, *Automation and the Library of Congress;* and Carl F.J. Overhage and R. Joyce Harman, eds., *INTREX.*

9. Stephen R. Salmon, *Library Automation Systems.*

10. Overhage and Harman, *INTREX.*

11. Edwin B. Parker, "Developing a Campus Information Retrieval System."

12. *Machine Readable Cataloging 1982-83, MARC Services, Cataloging Distribution Service,* pp. 3, 6.

13. In the following discussion, current data pertaining to the membership of OCLC and OCLC data base were supplied by Mary Ellen Jacob, director for Library Planning, OCLC, Inc. Telephone interview, June 1982.

14. Thomas B. Hickey and David J. Rypka, "Automatic Detection of Duplicate Monographic Records," pp. 125-142.

15. Susan K. Martin, *Library Networks 1976-77,* p. 34.

16. S. Michael Malinconico and Paul J. Fasana, *The Future of the Catalog,* p. 22.

17. In the following discussion, current data pertaining to the membership of RLG, to the non-RLG users of RLIN, and to the RLIN data base were supplied by Sarah E. Thomas, manager, Library Coordination, RLG, Inc. Telephone interview, June 1982.

18. In the following discussion, current data pertaining to the membership of WLN and its data base were supplied by Robert D. Payne, director, WLN. Telephone interview, June 1982.

19. For a more complete discussion, see Susan K. Martin, *Library Networks: 1981-82.*

20. *OCLC Newsletter,* March 1982, no. 140, p. 1; *OCLC Newsletter,* May 1981, no. 141, p. 3.

21. *OCLC Newsletter,* June 1981, no. 136, p. 1.

22. *OCLC Newsletter,* July 1980, no. 130, p. 1.

23. See G.C. Nielen, "Foundations for a Curriculum in 'Large Systems,'" pp. 169-175.

2 Profiles of the Case-Study Libraries

This chapter briefly describes our study participants, the libraries of the University of Chicago, Stanford University, Northwestern University, and the University of Washington. Each profile includes a table of organization, depicting the library's relationship to the host university and the location of the various divisions and departments. The profiles also highlight how different segments of the organization use and are affected by automated systems.

However, before setting forth on our tour of automation in four university libraries, we present in table 2–1 summary data characterizing each organization. The data describe the institutions for the academic year 1979–1980, the year in which the case studies were conducted. The library data for Northwestern do *not* include the university's dentistry, law, and medical libraries, none of which are located on the university's main campus in Evanston, Illinois.

Table 2–1
Summary Data 1978–1979

	Chicago	Stanford	Northwestern	University of Washington
A. *User communities*				
Undergraduate (full-time equivalents)	2,700	6,600	6,200	26,000
Graduate (full-time equivalents)	5,100	5,200	3,300	6,300
Faculty (full-time equivalents)	1,000	1,200	1,300	1,800
Degrees awarded	2,700	4,100	3,700	7,400
B. *Library expenditures*				
Total (millions)	$6.4	$12.7	$4.9	$9.3
Proportion of university budget	3.1%	3.6%	2.7%	2.2%

Table 2-1 continued

	Chicago	Stanford	Northwestern	University of Washington
C. *Allocation of library budget*				
Personnel	54%	60%	58%	58%
Materials	30%	31%	27%	31%
Operating	16%	9%	15%	11%
D. *Professional staff*	70	129	80	120
E. *Collection statistics*				
Size (millions)	4.2	4.5	2.1	3.8
Volumes added	160,000	135,000	65,000	184,000
Current serials	44,000	41,000	21,000	46,000
Interlibrary loans	22,000	21,400	4,200	110,000
Interlibrary borrows	5,700	3,800	2,400	5,200

When compared to those at the other sites, Chicago's collection size and growth rate seem outstanding relative to the size of its user community. This difference is due in part to Chicago's inclusion of microforms in its volume count; microforms are not included in the volume counts of the other institutions. It also reflects, though, the age of the university and a long and distinguished history of support for collection development.

As table 2-1 indicates, the University of Washington fulfills well over twice as many interlibrary-loan requests as do the other three institutions combined. This figure is consistent with our perception that public institutions play a much greater role in resource sharing than do private institutions.

The data in table 2-1 give only superficial information about each of the four libraries included in our case studies. For more detail, we turn now to individual profiles of each institution.

University of Chicago

For the University of Chicago library, the decade of the 1970s was one of change, often accompanied by turmoil. At the beginning of the decade, the library's director retired. A year later a new director, with a quite different management style, took the helm. In 1970, the main library moved to a new and much larger facility, the Regenstein Library. Over the next years, an organizational structure that had evolved to accommodate the structural constraints of the older facility had to adapt to different allocations and arrangements of space. At the same time, it had to assimilate new collections and staff, because eight branch libraries, previously housed in separate facilities, also moved to Regenstein.

The branch librarians joined the Regenstein staff as subject specialists responsible for collection development and reference services. The move forced them to relinquish the autonomy they had enjoyed as administrators of independent collections, an adjustment that was difficult for some. Their collection-development decisions had to be more closely coordinated with those of other librarians. Time allocation was now determined by the needs of the larger organization. Supervision, which they had been previously spared because of their relative invisibility, became a reality. The library experimented with a number of management schemes before it settled into one that effectively coordinated the activities of the once-independent branch librarians with those of the other public-service librarians in Regenstein. This experimentation caused a great deal of instability in the organization of public services.

A burgeoning fiscal crisis also contributed to changes in the organization of public services and other areas of the library as well. In the late 1960s and early 1970s, the library operated with what could be described as a comfortable budget. However, as with most other academic libraries, the fiscal situation of the Chicago library deteriorated as the decade wore on. Its budget held nearly constant in absolute terms, but the dollars available became less valuable because of inflation and unfavorable foreign-exchange rates. A number of positions were terminated or not refilled when vacated as a result of the financial crisis, their functions being abandoned or incorporated in other positions. Thus, the library's formal organization was often altered.

In 1971, an effort to unionize both professional and nonprofessional staff surfaced, stimulated by several factors, including hostility toward the library's management, frustration with poor communications resulting from an awkward organizational structure, and insecurity about job stability. Ultimately, the professional-staff union was refused certification by the National Labor Relations Board and the nonprofessional-union movement also faltered. However, the discord that inspired and deepened during the unionization effort lingered on. On a day in 1973 known as "Black Friday," six professional-librarian positions were eliminated as a result of budget cuts and a reorganization of public services. The following Monday, many members of the library staff participated in a one-day strike to protest the terminations.

Job insecurity at Chicago in the late 1960s and early 1970s had two sources. One was the changing fiscal situation. The other was a major automation project that promised to introduce computer-based support tools to all areas of library operation. Installation of these tools was accompanied by revisions in the organization of work and personnel, fundamental changes that the library had also to assimilate during the 1970s. Ironically, by the time the library's computer systems had evolved to the point of affecting the organization of work significantly, library staff were grateful for their introduction, for in some areas of the library the workload far exceeded staff resources, a situation forced by the budget crisis.

Chicago had begun in 1964 to explore systematically using computers in support of its operations. In 1966, it received funds from the National Science Foundation to develop a system that could support both technical services and circulation. The design effort was eventually focused on a system that could produce the various printed materials for which technical services is responsible: purchase orders, catalog cards, and book cards and pockets. The Book Processing System, as it was called, was developed and installed by 1968. It relied on the campus's central computer and on a combination of on-line and batch processing. The library was not able to begin work on circulation before its National Science Foundation funding ended in 1970.

A major concern in the design of the Book Processing System was determining the content of bibliographic records and defining the data fields for computer processing. In 1966 the specification of bibliographic records was receiving considerable national attention. The center of that attention was LC, where work was progressing on MARC. Much was being discussed and written about MARC, and Chicago gained from and contributed to those discussions. However, Chicago designed its records with little guidance from the final specifications of MARC records. The intent of the MARC project was to provide machine-readable catalog data. Chicago's system had the broader objective of supporting both acquisitions and cataloging. Although the problems confronted by the two projects overlapped, they were not identical; and this difference was reflected in the final content of their records. Furthermore, Chicago completed its design before the final specifications for MARC were released. Chicago would have had to delay further progress to allow for the possible incorporation of MARC conventions. When MARC was finally released, Chicago had already made substantial progress on the software to process its records.

Implementation of the Book Processing System involved almost no reorganization of work or personnel. A data-processing unit was created to handle all system interactions. The typing pool that previously had prepared purchase orders, catalog cards, and the like was disbanded. The only other change brought on by the system was a rechanneling of the data for record creation and requests for document production from the typing pool to the data-processing unit.

Several motives lay behind the decision to design and implement a system that had minimal effect upon the organization and operation of technical services. Change inevitably produces apprehension among staff, and especially in organizations that have experienced stability for some time. In 1966, the technical-services unit at Chicago was such a stable structure. The administration did not want to cope simultaneously with personnel and system-development problems; thus it sought a system that would affect the organization minimally.

Furthermore, in 1968 the personnel problems normally accompanying organizational change would have been aggravated by the particular type of change involved—automation. In the late 1960s, automation was viewed with both alarm and distrust. Automation meant loss of jobs, rigid adherence to rules and procedures, and unquestioned deference to a machine. Attempts to expound upon its positive aspects were perceived as propaganda. Hence, implementing a computer system in such an atmosphere was bound to be met by resistance and hostility.

An additional element in the decision not to restructure the existing organization was the anticipated cost of doing so. The system evolving at Chicago represented the state of the art in library computer systems. Considerable trial, error, and revision were anticipated. To integrate the system into the workflow of acquisitions and cataloging would have disrupted operations perhaps over an extended period. Finally, in 1966 the library was occupying a facility it had outgrown a half century earlier. Constraints on space severely limited the ways in which the system could have been more directly linked to technical-services activities.

In 1971, the library obtained funding from the National Endowment for the Humanities and the Council on Library Resources to continue its work on computer-based library systems. The project resulted in a considerably more sophisticated system for technical services, one that has been operating since 1974. The project also produced an on-line circulation system for the main-library collection, completed in 1978. The data files supporting the two systems were to be linked, but this goal was not achieved before external funding for development came to an end in 1978. The technical-services and circulation systems are referred to as one entity—the Library Data Management System (LDMS).

The campus's central computing facility is relied upon to provide the computing power for the LDMS. A minicomputer in the main library simultaneously supervises on-line interactions between some sixty library terminals and the campus computer through one communication line. In 1979, the LDMS was averaging 350,000 on-line transactions per month. The minicomputer also permits the library to use several different kinds of terminals by converting their data into a uniform code acceptable to the main computer.

As a result of operating the Book Processing System, the library accumulated a machine-readable file of on-order, in-process, and recently cataloged titles. However, the file was really a by-product of the system. Records could be retrieved only by a machine-generated number, a form of access that was sufficient for the purpose of generating printed products derived from given records but essentially useless for any other kind of data processing.

In contrast to the Book Processing System data base, the data base of the LDMS is its core. It centralizes and integrates almost all the information the library collects and processes relevant to its new books, serials, and other acquisitions, including their subsequent catalog records. Information about the library's users and the location of circulating titles is also part of the data base. The sixty cathode-ray terminals (CRTs) distribute access to the data base and eliminate the need to maintain the many paper files that previously stored and organized this information. The distributed-terminal network also allows information to be entered or updated in real-time by those responsible for maintaining the data. A sophisticated data-management system facilitates the building and maintenance of the files and the retrieval of data.

The major on-line data file in the technical-services subsystem of the LDMS is the Bibliographic Item File (BIF). It contains records for all items on-order or in-process, as well as records for all items cataloged since 1975. The content, data definitions, and structure of the BIF records are compatible with those of MARC. A file of the most recent fifteen to twenty-five weeks of LC MARC records is also maintained on-line. Records in the BIF and MARC files have several points of entry, including international standard-book and serial numbers and search codes derived from title and author entries and their combination. In addition, records in the BIF can be retrieved through the author, title, and subject entries normally associated with a card catalog, as well as through combinations of these entries.

On-line files of information pertinent to the processing of acquisitions are also part of the technical-services system. Pointers connect the records of one processing file to those of other processing files and to records in the BIF. For example, an order file is maintained, the records of which include an order number, the specifications of the order, and links to appropriate entries in a vendor file, a file of library book funds, a file of dates by which the material should be received, and the BIF. The multiple-file, linked-record structure of the LDMS minimizes redundancy in the stored information.

Two major technical-services files are maintained off-line for batch processing. One contains essentially all of Chicago's cataloging completed between 1968 and 1975. The other contains all those MARC records that have been received by Chicago but are not on-line. The earliest MARC records date back to 1971.

When the design of the technical-services system was essentially completed, work on the circulation system began. Its design and development were accompanied by broader staff involvement. Decisions concerning the technical-services system were for the most part those of the systems staff. In contrast, circulation staff joined the systems staff in the design and implementation of the circulation system. A change in the expectations of staff concerning their role in managing the affairs of the library was largely responsible for this difference.

In the wake of the unionization effort mentioned previously, the library's staff was deeply divided. Shortly after the demise of the effort, the library director initiated a program that he hoped would ease the tension among staff. The program, sponsored by the Industrial Relations Center, a research and development organization affiliated with the University of Chicago, introduced library staff to a form of participatory management. It established organizational structures through which staff could become involved in decision making. The center also conducted workshops to prepare staff to assume their new roles. The implementation of the technical-services system was well under way before the ethos of participation in decision making had taken hold. However, circulation's computerization was just getting started.

Actually, the mechanism through which circulation staff participated in the implementation was not a product of the center's program, although the program can be credited with influencing the type of mechanism the library selected. The initial plans for the circulation system encompassed the main library as well as its branches. The software required by a multiunit circulation system was within grasp. However, the hardware available to the library made it impossible to implement the system as widely as the library desired. The compromises forced by hardware limitations were not easily accepted by the systems department, and deadline after deadline passed without the promised system's emerging.

In preparation for the installation they thought was imminent, branch libraries allocated their limited staff resources to labeling books with the bar codes the system would use for identifying titles. Some branches started as early as 1973. With each new fiscal year, the library's management publicly announced that the library would shortly have its circulation system. In 1975, as the credibility of the administration and the systems department began to wane, an International Business Machines Corporation (IBM) consultant was hired to introduce a structured approach to design and development that demanded the participation of both circulation and systems staff. Through the procedures the consultant helped establish, and a scaling down of the original specifications, the circulation system was finally completed in 1978.

The system depends on bar-coded labels to identify users as well as books. The labels are read during loan transactions by a penlike object attached to each circulation terminal. The identification numbers enter an on-line loan file to form a record of the transaction.

The overall design of both the Book Processing System and the LDMS

has been the responsibility of the library's systems department. As figure
2-1 shows, the systems department reports to the director of the University
of Chicago library. In 1979, four staff members made up the department.
All have played major roles in the development of the LDMS. However, at
the time of our study, only two worked full-time on the system, reflecting
the rollback in funding for further development.

The design and programming of system components and their operation and maintenance are the responsibility of personnel from the campus's
computer center. This eight-member group resides organizationally within
the computer center but is housed in the library. While it was active, the
NEH/CLR grant supported the computer-center staff. Now the library supports them through its budget.

As figure 2-1 summarizes, the director's staff consists of an administrative services manager, a personnel officer, a development officer, and
the systems department. The head of administrative services works with the
director on budget planning. He monitors the library's expenditures. All
materials except books and serials are ordered through his office. His office
is also concerned with maintenance of the physical plant, shipping and
receiving, and the library's photoduplication activities. The development
officer initiates programs and contacts leading to contributions of money
and other gifts in support of the library.

There are four major operational units within the library: technical services, public services, special collections, and the law library. Within technical services, books and serials are processed separately. All serials processing is performed in one department, the serials department. The units
referred to as acquisitions and cataloging in figure 2-1 are responsible for
the nonserial formats, in particular, books. These two units are the primary
users of the LDMS technical-services system. Indeed, the activities engaged
in by the acquisitions and cataloging departments are those the system was
intended to support. Correspondingly, the book-processing departments
have been the only units to undergo substantial changes in the way their
work is organized and conducted as a result of the technical-services system.
Their operations are now so dependent on the LDMS that when it stops
functioning, many book-processing activities also halt.

The acquisitions and cataloging departments are responsible for almost
all data entry into and update of the Bibliographic Item File. Data input is
facilitated by screens that prompt for the required information and error-
detection routines that alert staff when the data do not conform to specified
standards. Staff in acquisitions initiate BIF records, including those
representing material acquired through gifts and through standing order
and approval plans. Before a record is created, acquisitions staff must
check to see if the library already has or may soon have the material or some
current edition of it. This process involves searching order informa-

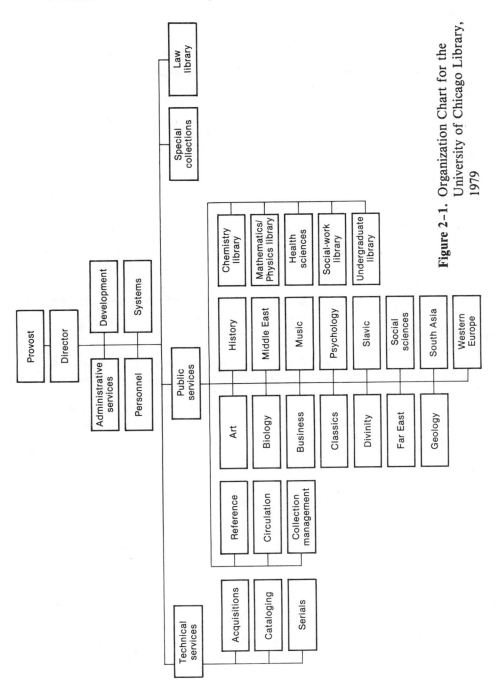

Figure 2-1. Organization Chart for the University of Chicago Library, 1979

tion, books-in-process data, and catalog records. For current imprints, staff need only search the BIF. As was mentioned before, the BIF contains all order and in-process information and all cataloging performed since 1975. For older titles, staff must also search the public card catalog.

Acquisitions staff include in BIF records LC catalog data, if they are available. The sources pursued are the National Union Catalog, a depository card file, and the MARC on-line and off-line files. Records retrieved from the MARC files can simply be merged into the BIF. Delays in LC cataloging often result in LC records appearing after a title has completed acquisitions processing. Each new MARC tape received by the library is matched against the BIF to retrieve those MARC records of on-order or in-process titles for which LC data have not been found previously. For titles outside of MARC's scope, hardcopy sources may be pursued again—but by staff in the catalog department.

Within the catalog department, two groups catalog new acquistions. One works solely with material accompanied by LC catalog records. The other handles selected LC cataloging copy but primarily is concerned with titles for which no LC records can be expected in the time desired by the library. As is common in academic libraries, members of the former group are referred to as *copy catalogers,* and those in the latter group, *original catalogers.* All professional librarians in the cataloging department are original catalogers.

In research libraries, cataloging is the bottleneck of material processing, especially for books requiring original cataloging. Few libraries can afford to allocate to their catalog departments the resources required to keep up with the flow of uncataloged material. At Chicago, for example, original catalogers are able to complete an average of three to four records a day for titles with no LC catalog copy. The department daily receives an average of fifty-six books for which no copy has been uncovered. A staff of sixteen original catalogers would be needed to prevent the backup of these books, a luxury the library cannot afford.

As has been suggested previously, cataloging that is based on a record produced by another library using similar cataloging practices takes considerably less time than cataloging without such a record. For example, Chicago can complete the records of four titles accompanied by LC catalog data in the time that it takes to complete one without LC copy. Such time savings encourage libraries to wait for other institutions to catalog titles if there is some reason to expect that other institutions will do so. At Chicago, most books leaving acquisitions without LC catalog records are held in what is called a *W-collection.* Here they may reside for up to five years, retrieved before then if LC catalog records are uncovered or if a special reason, such as a user request, emerges for making them part of the cataloged collection. In 1979, the W-collection contained 35,000 titles.

The LDMS supports cataloging primarily by providing new and making more efficient previously used ways to exploit LC cataloging. For example, when a MARC record is used, it can be transferred directly into the BIF. No time must be allocated to transcription or for proofreading. Also, the LDMS scans new MARC tapes for titles in the W-collection that are represented in the BIF, providing another time savings for cataloging personnel.

The system does little to aid the process of original cataloging. In fact, it has complicated the task somewhat. Now catalogers must prepare information in a form acceptable to the computer—adding to the tasks of upgrading existing data and creating bibliographic data the additional task of properly tagging and coding the data.

The tasks of serials processing and book processing overlap, but not entirely. Because of the continuing receipt of a serial, serials processing is more complicated. The technical-services component of the LDMS was designed to handle books. It was being used by the serials department but only to support its booklike tasks. In particular, the serials department entered its order and catalog data and thus maintained an on-line file of its in-process and recently cataloged titles. This procedure facilitated preorder searching and provided data to generate purchase orders and catalog cards. It also allowed the department to rely on the LDMS's automatic monitoring of dates by which orders are expected to arrive. However, the system could only be used to check the receipt of the first issue of a serial. Monitoring receipt of later issues was still a manual task.

The LDMS was not useful as a tool to retrieve LC serials cataloging. LC separately issued its cataloging of books and serials. The latter file is known as MARC-S. Chicago subscribed to the MARC-S service, but the data were not available for machine searching. At the time of our study, work was in progress to remedy this situation.

Since 1975, serials known to have MARC copy have not received complete cataloging. About one-third of the titles received for cataloging fall into this group. Each is documented in the public catalog, but by an abbreviated record that is retrievable only through its title. The cost of keying-in and proofreading the data is responsible for this policy. When the MARC-S tapes are finally available, the records representing these titles will be copied into the BIF and full catalog-card sets will be generated. The serials department intends to accept the LC data without revision.

A similar policy was employed in book cataloging for titles with MARC records issued before 1976. The tapes containing these records were not available until 1979, by which time the card-production backlog had gathered more than ten thousand titles. As expected, the system quickly generated the required card sets. However, filing the cards that inundated the library was a problem. For months, trays of cards lay ready for filing, waiting for the staff the library could devote to them.

Public services at Chicago contains twenty-three units, located within and outside of the main library. Those outside of Regenstein are system branches, including the undergraduate and medical-school libraries and libraries supporting social-services administration, chemistry, mathematics, and physics. Public-service departments within the main library are circulation, reference, collection development, and fifteen units representing discrete collections administered by subject specialists.

The collections of Regenstein are organized around discipline-oriented reading rooms that are distributed throughout the seven-floored structure. The collections relevant to each discipline are filed near the reading rooms, and subject specialists maintain offices in the same area. The specialists primarily are responsible for managing the reading rooms and their corresponding collections and helping those who use them. The maintenance of discrete collections reflects the former status of branch units that have merged with the main collection. Originally, the subject specialists were branch librarians. However, through the years some of the individuals in these roles have changed, as has the mix of subject expertise.

Formally, the head of public services directly supervises all twenty-three public-service departments, an exceptionally large span of control in any organization. In practice, however, the collection-development officer and the heads of circulation and reference assume part of the supervisory responsibility. They each chair committees through which policy for the areas they represent is established and carried out.

The public-service units encompass almost all the library's collections. The exceptions are special collections and the law library, which are within the library system but outside of the control of the head of public services. These units report to the library director. The collections administered within public services are developed by the division's subject specialists, who are also called *bibliographers*, the collection-development officer, branch librarians, and reference librarians.

When a new MARC tape is received, the LDMS sorts its records by LC classification and prints a sorted set of records for distribution to selectors, each of whom is assigned specific LC ranges. The slips are used to alert selectors to possible acquisitions within their areas of responsibility.

The LDMS is also used directly by selectors to help them with collection development. However, selectors have limited access to the system, which in turn limits its usefulness. Some thirty terminals are located in public services, but twenty-six are in the circulation department. Among the branches, only the physics/mathematics library has a terminal. The remaining terminals are located in the reference department and on two of the library's upper floors.

The branch, reference, and floor terminals are also used to help answer the questions of library users. The reference department is most dependent on the system for this aspect of its aid. For about one in three questions, reference librarians use the terminal. Logs of reference activity indicate that about 15 percent of the questions can be answered completely only with the use of the LDMS. These questions pertain primarily to the on-order and in-process data.

The reference department and the chemistry library offer on-line searching of the Lockheed and SDC data bases. The chemistry library is responsible for the science bases. The humanities and social-science bases are the domain of reference. The Lockheed and SDC service has been provided by reference since 1979 and by the chemistry library since 1978. Actually, the chemistry-library service grew out of a search service started several years earlier by the chemistry department. It was transferred to the library when the chemistry department decided it could no longer afford it.

Thirty-five staff members make up the circulation department, not all of whom, though, work full-time. A number of students are also employed by circulation, each working ten to fifteen hours a week. They are assigned primarily to labor-intensive activities of charging, discharging, and shelving books, and also monitoring the library's entrances. The latter involves checking the identification of the six-thousand to seven-thousand people who daily enter Regenstein.

The circulation staff are organized into six sections, covering the circulation activities described in chapter 1 as well as graduate reserves and entrance/exit control. *Graduate reserves* is a discrete collection of materials placed on reserve by professors for their graduate-level courses. Its circulation is administered separately from that of the general collection; however, it is supported by the LDMS. In fact, the system has been supporting the circulation of reserved material since 1976. Graduate reserves was selected as the test site for the circulation software.

Circulating a collection is an activity laden with numerous high-volume tasks. For example, in the 1977–1978 fiscal year, 800,000 items were shelved by the personnel responsible for maintaining the stacks. During that year, some 300,000 titles from the general collection were lent to users, some 300,000 returned, and some 200,000 renewed. Prior to the LDMS, a paper file containing on the average 120,000 slips documented these transactions. On a daily basis, 900 records needed to be added, 900 withdrawn, and 600 updated.

The LDMS has eased the burden of many circulation tasks. First and foremost, the transaction file is now machine-readable and on-line. The computer assumes the chore of record filing and retrieval. Some tasks that were difficult and sometimes impossible to complete under the manual system are now regularly accomplished by the system. For example, the circulation department had great difficulty keeping up with overdue material. Leafing through the loan file in search of overdues consumed a great deal of time. Now the department can rely entirely on the LDMS to alert it to overdue material. Also, the computer automatically blocks a charge if the individual's identification number has been flagged. For example, his privileges may be withdrawn because of abuse. Although it was possible before the LDMS, blocking was considerably more awkward and less effective.

The circulation staff are responsible for handling all charges and discharges. However, a self-service terminal allows users to renew their loans without staff intervention, easing the volume of counter activity. The LDMS generates the products of circulation activities. Overdue notices and recall slips are printed in batches. On-line transactions generate charge, discharge, and renewal slips.

Stanford University

The director of the Stanford University libraries reports to the office of the provost. The system he administers includes the central Green Library, which houses the general collections and administrative offices, the undergraduate library, and ten departmental libraries, the latter serving art and architecture, education, music, biology, chemistry and chemical engineering, earth sciences, engineering, marine biology, mathematics and computer science, and physics. Reading rooms are also part of the system, although their staff and acquisitions are paid for by the departments they serve. Most depend on system resources for the technical processing of their acquisitions though not for guidance in the development of their collections.

Our field work concentrated on the units of the central-library system and excluded six major campus libraries that are not part of the system: the libraries of the business, law, and medical schools; those of the Food Research Institute; the Hoover Institution on War, Revolution, and Peace; and the Stanford Linear Accelerator Center. Each of these *coordinate libraries,* as they are called, is administered by the organization of which it is a part. When we refer to the *library,* we shall mean the central-library system.

This central system and nearly all the coordinate libraries participate in the Research Libraries Information Network. As has been mentioned previously, RLIN is the computer-based communication system operated by the Research Libraries Group, of which Stanford is a member. Although the members of RLG share equally in the ownership of RLIN, the Stanford University Libraries have a unique position within the group. RLG is located on the Stanford campus; the RLIN computer is housed in the university's computer center and maintained by computer-center staff; and, perhaps most importantly, Stanford developed the system upon which RLIN is based, BALLOTS.

The Stanford University libraries began project BALLOTS (Bibliographic Automation of Large Library Operations using a Timesharing System) in 1967, with funding from the Office of Education. An automation department was created, charged with analyzing library operations and developing system requirements. The library did not staff it with software designers and programmers. The university's computer center was relied on for such technical expertise.

In 1968, a single development manager was given responsibility for BALLOTS and SPIRES, a project of Stanford's Institute for Communication Research, financed by the National Science Foundation. The intent of SPIRES (Stanford Physics Information Retrieval System) was to build an on-line retrieval system for scientists, with a data base of records representing scientific documents. BALLOTS was to be an interactive system supporting the file-oriented activities of technical services and eventually circulation. Both systems required software that would allow the simultaneous processing of large data files in real-time by numerous users. They also required software to facilitate the creation and maintenance of data files and the retrieval and reformatting of the content of file records. Acceptable software meeting these requirements was not commercially available. Rather than develop such software independently, it was decided that project funds would be spent more effectively if the management of the two research and development projects was centralized. The goal of the SPIRES component of the merged projects was to build a generalized file-management system, while BALLOTS developed specific acquisition and cataloging applications.

Prototypes of BALLOTS and SPIRES emerged in 1969 for a brief period of evaluation. The BALLOTS model supported the acquisition of monographs and operated for nine months, during which time two on-line files were created. One contained order data for a portion of the titles acquired during the model's demonstration and the other contained MARC records. The system generated purchase orders, claim and cancellation notices, and other acquisitions-related documents.

During the model's run, manual acquisitions procedures continued without change. Like Chicago, Stanford created a special data-processing unit to handle all system transactions—and for many of the same reasons. However, one of the conclusions of the evaluation was that the full effect of BALLOTS on improving operations could only be realized if those who built, maintained, and used its data files worked directly with the system. BALLOTS's next generation was intended for integration into the workplace.

In 1970, the BALLOTS and SPIRES projects reassumed complete independence at the managerial level, and the director of libraries assigned daily administration of the BALLOTS unit to the director of the computation center. The library directly determined project priorities and system specifications, and the director of libraries continued as a principal investigator for fund-raising proposals. However, the library became functionally a client contracting the center to develop a system. All staff formally assigned to the project were computer-center employees, except for the project manager, who held a joint appointment with the library and the computer center.

After the split, SPIRES evolved into a software project also located within the computer center, severing its ties with the institute. The goal of the software project was to improve and further generalize SPIRES information-retrieval software. Throughout their development, BALLOTS and, later, RLIN have relied on SPIRES to provide the underlying data-management component of their software.

The Office of Education funding for BALLOTS ended in 1971. Over the next year, BALLOTS's development was supported by the university. In 1972, the library obtained a two-year grant from the National Endowment for the Humanities and the Council on Library Resources to continue with BALLOTS's development. By late 1974, BALLOTS's second generation was firmly in place, supporting the acquisition and cataloging of monographs. All new book orders were being recorded in the system, as was about 80 percent of new cataloged records. From the data, BALLOTS produced purchase orders, claims, cancellations, catalog cards, and various other technical-services documents.

Motivated in part by a desire to recover some of BALLOTS's operating costs, Stanford decided to extend the use of the system to other libraries. In 1974, the California State Library granted Stanford funds to develop an expanded cataloging support module to be made available to seven of the state's public libraries as a first step toward a Public Library Automation Network (PLAN). In 1975, the Council on Library Resources granted Stanford funds to further extend BALLOTS within the state of California. By 1976, the networking of BALLOTS had gone beyond California's libraries to include public, special, and academic libraries in other states. However, the anticipated financial gains in networking BALLOTS were not realized. Because it wished to remain competitive with OCLC, BALLOTS was not able to recover completely the cost of providing services to its users. The pricing policy brought the BALLOTS project greater involvement of the university administration, which began to explore alternatives for BALLOTS's future, including its possible termination.

The Research Libraries Group was formed in 1975 by the Columbia, Harvard, New York Public, and Yale libraries. Its goals were to increase mutual access to the members' bibliographic data and material resources and to coordinate a number of costly activities, including preservation of their holdings and collection development. A computer-based communication system was thought essential to achieving these goals. In 1977, the Research Libraries Group evaluated several computer-based library systems in search of a facility to support its cooperative programs. The RLG's interest in BALLOTS as the system's foundation provided Stanford's administration with a justification to continue BALLOTS's support, at least until RLG made a decision. In fact, the administration encouraged BALLOTS's adoption by RLG in several ways, including reorganizing the project to facilitate its acquisition by an external agent. In the fall of 1977, the unit within the computer center responsible for BALLOTS became an independent organization, under the direction of the associate-provost. Shortly afterward, BALLOTS was adopted by RLG. BALLOTS was renamed RLIN upon its acquisition by RLG. Since the inititation of RLIN, RLG membership has steadily grown. As was mentioned earlier, it now stands at twenty-six.

Since our study of the Stanford library, RLIN's software and hardware have been considerably upgraded and its services expanded through more than ten million dollars in grants and loans from foundations and RLG members. It also experienced considerable organizational and operational turbulence.[1] However, our concern here is with describing conditions as they were in mid-1979, and, in particular, focusing on RLIN as it was used by the Stanford University libraries at that time.

RLIN's on-line data base at the time contained almost two-million records, held in four files. Library of Congress MARC monographic records issued since 1972 made up what was called the MARC file. The Catalog Data File (CDF) contained cataloging records generated by RLIN users. Almost all of the monographic titles cataloged by Stanford since 1972 were represented in this file. The Reference File was composed of *see, see also,* and explanatory cross-references to Stanford's CDF records. The Stanford library was the only RLIN user that could make entries into the Reference File. It also was the only library entering records into the In-Process File (IPF), a file containing bibliographic as well as order data for titles on order or awaiting cataloging. Both the reference and acquisitions components of RLIN were those developed for the Stanford library as part of the BALLOTS project. Neither had been generalized for use by other RLIN participants.

Several different indexes provided entry to the on-line files, including personal name, corporate or conference name, and title. For all these, significant words could be sought, except for extremely common words like *bulletin* and *institute.* Subject, call number, International Standard Book Number (ISBN), LC card number, and RLIN identification-number indexes were also maintained. Not all indexes operated over all the files. The CDF indexes included all but the ISBN number. The IPF could not be searched via call number, subject, or ISBN. The MARC-file indexes were personal name, corporate or conference name, title, LC card number, and ISBN. Index entries could be combined for more focused searching. Also, search requests could be stored in what was called a Standing Search Request (SSR) file. Stored requests were automatically run each month against the MARC file, which weekly received new LC records.

We now turn to a description of the organization of the central-library system, including in our discussion a summary of how RLIN was being used by the system's various units. Figure 2-2 provides an organization chart for the library. Units that serve in a staff capacity to the director include administrative services, building projects, and personnel. The university archivist also reports to the director. At the time of our study, the main concern of building projects was a major new addition to the Green Library. Its construction was nearing completion, and final plans were being made for the library's occupation of the new space.

Administrative services encompasses budget control, procurement of materials and equipment, and the library's duplication facilities. The development officer is located within this unit. Also reporting to the head of administrative services is the systems librarian, the principal liaison between the library and RLIN.

The position of systems librarian was at the time of our visit a relatively recent addition to the library's organization. The library released staff from their formally assigned responsibilities to work part-time on BALLOTS throughout its development. However, it was assumed that those released would reassume their former roles once their BALLOTS-related assignments concluded. From this group, one person emerged as a natural candidate for a full-time role in systems-related activities. This choice was owed to her extensive experience with the system, her long acquaintance with RLIN staff and RLIN's organization, and her intrinsic interest in computer-based systems. In 1978, she was therefore named systems librarian, leaving the position of government-documents cataloger. In fact, she had given much of her time to various aspects of BALLOTS's development and integration into library operations since 1974.

At first, the position of systems librarian was located within technical services, the original focus of BALLOTS activity and the organizational home of the cataloger given the position. However, because RLIN, too, was used by public-service units, the administration later decided to locate the systems function in an area of the library that represented more equally the interests of technical- and non-technical-services staff. In fact, at the time of our study, the library was considering hiring another systems librarian with a public-service background to improve the balance in the library's systems function.

Operations at Stanford are divided into three major components: technical services, public services, and collection management. As at Chicago,

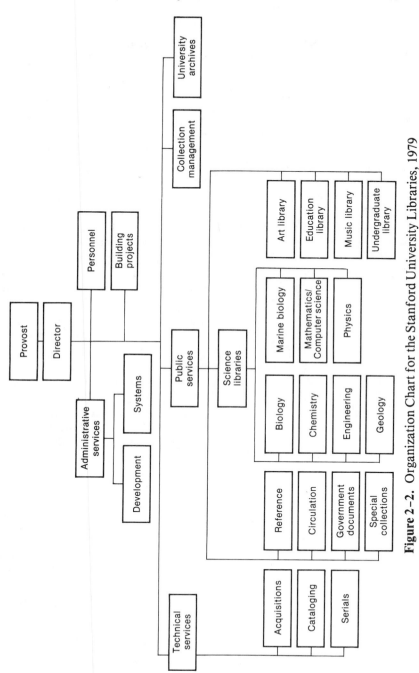

Figure 2-2. Organization Chart for the Stanford University Libraries, 1979

the processing of serials is organizationally separated from the processing of other materials. The acquisitions and cataloging departments noted in figure 2–2 attend to nonserial titles; acquisition and cataloging of serials are performed by the serials department.

Systemwide book cataloging is centralized in the technical-services division but shared by the acquisitions and cataloging departments. The titles cataloged by acquisitions must have MARC catalog data available when they are received. Additional criteria further restrict the titles the acquisitions department catalogs. In fact, at the time of our study, less than 5 percent of all books cataloged were done in acquisitions. However, its involvement in cataloging had just begun, and its role was expected to expand because of the efficiency gained in having books cataloged by the unit that receives them.

The Library of Congress has issued formats for the machine-readable catalog records of books, serials, films, manuscripts, maps and music. The formats differ, reflecting the variation in the characteristics of the various types of material. Chicago's LDMS could accommodate the differences in record format. However, at the time of our study, RLIN could process only the book format. Thus, in mid-1979, RLIN's cataloging support theoretically encompassed only books. Nonetheless, Stanford was using RLIN to catalog its serials, adapting its serials cataloging to fit the conventions of book format. A major system enhancement was, however, about to change Stanford's treatment of serials cataloging.

During our field work, RLG was developing a new module to support serials cataloging in RLIN. In fact, both Stanford and the University of California at Berkeley (UCB) were placing serials catalog records for both their ceased and continuing subscriptions into the file that would become the CDF for serials when the new module was finally available. At Stanford, records of new serials were also entering the CDF for books because card production was not yet available for records in the serials file.

The Stanford and UCB conversion efforts were funded by a U.S. Office of Education grant that also included the University of California at Los Angeles (UCLA). The intent of the project was to build a union list of the campuses' serials holdings that would be disseminated nationally in microform. While Stanford and UCB were using RLIN as the repository for their data, UCLA was using OCLC. All the data would eventually be merged into one machine-readable file.

As can be seen in figure 2–2, all branch libraries of the central system report to the associate director for public services. The science branches form what is called the *science department* and report to the public-services director through a coordinator, who also heads the engineering library.

The undergraduate library is unique among the Stanford libraries in that it has never had a traditional card catalog. When the library opened in

1966, its catalog was in book form, catalog data being stored in machine-readable punched cards, which were used to produce the book catalog. In 1974 a conversion project moved the data base into the on-line CDF, which thereafter became the recipient of the undergraduate library's catalog data. At present essentially all the library's holdings are represented on-line, another feature that distinguishes the undergraduate library from other library units. In 1978, the undergraduate library began producing its catalog in microfiche rather than book format to save the cost of printing and binding and to decrease the time required for producing the catalog and its supplements.

Also within public services are the following departments of the central library: circulation, general reference, government documents, and special collections. When we conducted our study, circulation at Stanford was a completely manual system. One of the original goals of BALLOTS had been to provide computer support for this function. However, work on circulation never progressed beyond a preliminary specification phase. Efficient operation of Stanford's manual circulation system is highly dependent upon users' filling out the multicopy forms legibly. The library administration was anxious to replace the system but had no immediate plans for doing so. It had evaluated some turnkey commercial systems, several of which seemed nearly adequate but excessively costly. It was expected that the library eventually would acquire an already-developed system that operated on a locally maintained minicomputer. The library did not intend to develop its own system. Furthermore, RLG had no immediate plans to extend RLIN services into the area of circulation.

The general-reference department coordinates the library's on-line search service, offering the data bases available through DIALOG. Until 1979, essentially all commercial data-base searching within the central system was performed by one general-reference librarian. In 1979, the library decentralized the retrieval activity. The general-reference department now assumes primary responsibility for DIALOG's social-science and humanities data bases; however, searches requested by students and faculty from the School of Education are handled directly by the education library. The science and technical data bases have become the responsibility of the science branches.

Before the decentralization, there was little demand for data-base retrieval from students and faculty in the sciences. The science department hoped to spark demand by actively promoting a current-awareness program wherein the research interests of scientists would be translated into search profiles stored within the DIALOG system and automatically searched against new entries to prespecified data bases.

The collection-management office at Stanford reports to the director of libraries. An associate director heads the office and is responsible for supervising the collection-development activities of twenty-six librarians situated in other departments, as well as the four bibliographers who reside within the collection-management office. The director also acts as a bibliographer, managing specific areas of the main collection.

When our study was undertaken, the need for RLIN's support exceeded its availability. Some public-service units had no terminal link to RLIN, and in some departments with terminals, including all the technical-service departments, additional terminals would have immediately assumed full-time operation. Twenty-five terminals were distributed across the system, two-thirds used primarily the technical-service activities. Three of these technical-service terminals were located outside of the technical-service division. They were in the collection-management office, the government-documents department, and the undergraduate library. The collection-management and government-documents terminals were used to support preorder searching, to enter records into the in-process file, to request purchase orders derived from these records, and to monitor the status of materials on order. Both collection management and government documents, in effect, maintained acquisitions operations parallel to those maintained in the serials and acquisitions departments of technical services. The technical-services terminal in the undergraduate library was used primarily to support the processing activities of the undergraduate-reserves unit.

The undergraduate library had another terminal, a public-service terminal, installed at its reference desk. Public-service terminals were also located in the biology, chemistry, education, engineering, and music branches, and in the general-reference department of the Green Library. Public-service terminals differed from technical-service terminals in that they did not allow record creation or modification. The general-reference department had had its terminal since 1974, although most of the public-service terminals were installed in 1978.

As with the LDMS, RLIN had become an essential tool at the reference desk of the general-reference department. Other public-service sites with access to RLIN, especially the science branches, were much less dependent on the system to support their reference tasks. This situation may have existed because, when we visited Stanford, RLIN was still a novelty in the science units and had not yet been integrated fully into their reference functions. To be sure, it may also reflect different patterns of use between those in the humanities and social sciences and those in the sciences. The latter depend primarily on journal articles. They less frequently pursue questions that would initiate a search through the records of titles-in-process or a check of the catalog-data file for titles in a specific subject area.

The RLIN system offered little support to collection management beyond its documentation of recently cataloged titles and titles-in-process. Outside of the collection-management office, RLIN was not being used to support the intellectual aspects of collection development. The collection-management office was involved in an extensive evaluation program in which the library's holdings were being checked against scholarly bibliographies. The RLIN system was aiding the search through Stanford's holdings, although, of course, only those titles cataloged since 1972 were represented in the data base.

The clerical tasks of acquisitions were facilitated by the system. For item selectors with convenient access to RLIN, the system was relied upon to check that their orders were properly submitted by acquisitions staff in technical services, to monitor the status of their orders, and to determine the location in the technical-services workflow of titles that had been received by the library.

To avoid duplicate holdings, all item selectors participated to some extent in searching library files. Those with access to RLIN used it to check pending orders and the library's more recent acquisitions. RLIN was particularly useful to science selectors for preorder searching. Before RLIN, the science units had had convenient access only to their own pending orders and holdings. Union listings had been kept in the central library. With RLIN, a science unit had immediate access to the item-selection decisions and recently cataloged titles in all the other science branches. Most titles acquired by science branches are in any event recent publications; thus, RLIN's files were often the only source that needed to be checked.

As mentioned before, the collection-management office and the government-documents department bypass the preorder search and the order functions of technical services to acquire their material directly. These departments account for nearly one-third of the orders entering the in-process file. The serials and acquisitions departments are responsible for the remaining entries.

The acquisitions activities of collection development and government documents highlight the uncertainty in the functional boundaries that define a library's departments and divisions. Within university libraries in general, clerical tasks of acquisitions are performed by both item selectors and those who staff the acquisitions function of technical services. Acquisitions tasks undertaken by item selectors seldom are prescribed and cannot be counted on by staff in technical services to be performed regularly, confusing the boundaries of responsibility.

Cataloging provides another example of a function often distributed across library units. At Stanford, cataloging is for the most part centralized in technical services. However, many university libraries funnel only mainstream acquisitions to their central catalog department, leaving the cataloging of materials like sound recordings, technical reports, and rare books to specialists located in the units that house the materials. At Stanford, the specialty units reside organizationally in the central cataloging department.

Stanford has, however, moved some of the responsibility of cataloging into acquisitions, as we described earlier.

Northwestern University

The library resources of Northwestern are distributed between the university's two campus locations, Evanston and Chicago, Illinois. The core of Northwestern's academic program is in Evanston. In Evanston are also Northwestern's main library, housing titles in the humanities and social sciences, and branch libraries in geology, mathematics, music, transportation, and science and engineering. On the Chicago campus, twelve miles south of Evanston, are four additional libraries. One supports the campus's evening division and its program in management studies. The others support programs in dentistry, law, and medicine. The librarians heading the dentistry, law, and medicine libraries report to the deans of their respective schools. The business and evening-division library and all library units on the Evanston campus make up Northwestern's main library system. They are under the direction of the university librarian, who reports to the provost. The focus of our investigation was the main library system, the organizational structure of which is summarized in figure 2–3.

Many units of the main library system used computerized tools. Three terminals with attached printers, located in the reference department, the transportation library, and the science and engineering library, are dedicated to on-line searching of commercially supplied data bases. Cathode-ray terminals, installed throughout the main library and in the music, transportation, and science and engineering branches, are linked to circulation and technical-services support systems.

The circulation and technical-services systems were developed internally. Although they function independently, they form what is called the Northwestern On-line Total Integrated System (NOTIS). At the time of our study, NOTIS's software operated on the university's administrative data-processing computer facility. Shortly after our visit to Northwestern, the library obtained a dedicated IBM 4331 computer.

A linked-record design characterizes NOTIS's technical-services data base. The data base contains over 500,000 on-line bibliographic records, representing all the library's periodicals and essentially all monographs acquired since 1970. The data fields in a bibliographic record and their format match those of LC MARC records. For newly ordered or received titles, in fact, Northwestern creates preliminary catalog records by copying MARC cataloging into its data base when it is available. The library subscribes to both the serials and monograph tape services of LC. The tapes are maintained off-line and searched on a batch basis.

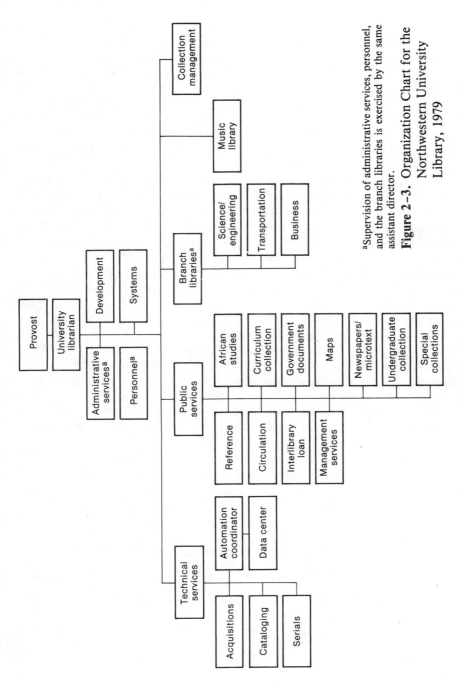

[a]Supervision of administrative services, personnel, and the branch libraries is exercised by the same assistant director.

Figure 2–3. Organization Chart for the Northwestern University Library, 1979

Attached to each bibliographic record is a *holdings record.* The holdings record notes the copies of a title owned by the library, giving each copy's location and call number. For serials, a holdings record details the volumes shelved at the cited locations. Linked to each copy specified in a holdings record are *order records,* describing all the various orders that have been initiated concerning the copy. An order record carries the following kinds of data: the vendor to whom the order was sent; the date by which the title or, in the case of a serial, the next piece of the title should be received; the price of the order; and the library fund from which payment is being or has been drawn.

Order records are designed to permit the entry of issues of a serial that have been received by the library but have not yet been included in a bound volume. This information provides the core data for NOTIS's automatic monitoring of the receipt of serials, a capability that neither the LDMS nor RLIN had at the time of our study. On a daily basis, NOTIS alerts library staff to missing issues. Notification is triggered by the passage of dates by which the pieces are expected to arrive, dates that have been explicitly set by library staff or algorithmically calculated by the computer on the basis of previous publication patterns. The system also generates, on request, claims for dispatch to vendors.

The on-line data base of the circulation support system is an exception file. It identifies those items not in their proper shelf location. Within an entry, the only data given about a title is its call number, which limits the services the circulation-system supports. For example, the computer-generated recall notices identify titles by call number rather than by title, something users find annoying. The circulation data base is considerably smaller than the technical-services base. At peak times the circulation file contains at most 80,000 entries.

Planning for NOTIS began in 1967 when the library hired a full-time systems analyst. Shortly after this addition a professor from the computer-science department began to devote part of his time to implementing support tools for the library. Circulation, which was installed in 1970, was his first operating system. A year later an interim technical-processing system was in place. This version was enhanced considerably in 1977.

Northwestern did not formally establish a systems department until 1973. The computer-science faculty member heads the unit, maintaining a joint appointment with the library and the computer-science department. He and the systems analyst were joined in 1977 by a full-time programmer. Two additional people, a systems analyst and a programmer, were added in 1980. Systems staff are responsible for the maintenance and enhancement of NOTIS, including all software design, redesign, and programming. As can be seen in figure 2–3, the systems department reports to the library director.

Also reporting directly to the university librarian are five assistant university librarians, covering the areas of development, technical services, public services, administrative services, and collection management. The development office was created in 1975 to centralize library activities related to fund-raising programs and grant proposals. In recent years, the library has enjoyed well over two million dollars in income beyond the budgeted funds it receives from the university. Sources have included foreign and U.S. government agencies, private foundations, corporations, and individuals.

As can be seen in figure 2–3, technical services at Northwestern include the traditional activities entailed in the processing of monographs and serials. Both acquisitions and cataloging are performed in two departments. The acquisitions department is concerned with acquiring monographs and nonperiodical serials. The material handled by this department is cataloged by the catalog department. The serials department acquires and catalogs all periodicals.

The technical-services components of NOTIS play an integral role in the operations of the technical-services units. NOTIS is the repository for nearly all the data they create about the titles they handle. It generates purchase orders, claim notices, catalog cards, book-labeling materials, and the machine-readable book-identification cards required by the circulation system. On a continuing basis, it performs a number of clerical tasks. For example, it automatically searches newly received MARC tapes for titles that have been previously but unsuccessfully sought on MARC. Based on programmed algorithms, it generates *action dates*, the dates by which monographs or pieces of serials should be received. If receipt of a title or one of its parts is not recorded in NOTIS before the action date is reached, the system generates a notification to alert staff.

The acquisitions units initiate new NOTIS records. They are called *provisional catalog records* and include all the bibliographic data acquisitions staff are able to uncover. The cataloging units do not engage in further searching beyond that performed by acquisitions. However, NOTIS's ongoing search of newly received MARC tapes may capture a catalog record for a title that has been passed on to the catalog department.

The cataloging units complete the provisional records built by acquisitions staff. Within the catalog department, one group, copy cataloging, attends to those records of monographs for which LC cataloging has been found. It generates about 90 percent of the catalog department's monographic cataloging. The remaining 10 percent is supplied by the original cataloging unit. This group typically works with titles for which no LC catalog data have been uncovered. The time required by original catalogers to complete a catalog record varies tremendously, from several minutes to several days. Factors responsible for this variation include the language of the work, its subject area, the complexity of the title's content, its length, and the quality of catalog data created by libraries other than the LC, when such data are available.

The serials-cataloging unit within the serials department attends to the catalog records of some monographic series as well as periodicals. About half of its cataloging is based on LC catalog records.

In addition to the acquisitions, cataloging, and serials department, the technical-services division includes the data center. When the acquisitions and cataloging components of NOTIS were first implemented, the library had only seven terminals in technical services. Two were housed in the serials department. The remaining five were grouped in a room adjacent to both the cataloging and acquisitions departments, which became known as the data center. It was hoped that the centralization of terminals would insure their full-time use and minimize the workflow problems in cataloging and acquisitions stemming from the limited number of terminals.

In 1971 the data center supported four full-time terminal operators, who shared the data-center terminals with acquisitions and cataloging staff. In addition to special projects, the terminal operators completed tasks that were part of the day-to-day workflow in acquisitions and cataloging. They, for example, searched the MARC data tapes for LC cataloging, input catalog data prepared by original catalogers, and requested claim notices for ordered titles that had not been received by monographic acquisitions. Since 1971 the library has added some sixteen terminals to technical services, installing them directly in the acquisitions and cataloging departments. The decentralization of data entry and retrieval sites has been accompanied by changes in the responsibilities of data-center-terminal operators. At the time of our study, the data center still housed five terminals. However, only two terminal operators remained on its staff, and one worked part-time. The positions lost by the data center have been taken on by the acquisitions and cataloging departments. Some technical-services staff members believe that the data center's role in data manipulation eventually will be limited to special projects or perhaps even be completely assumed by the other technical-services departments.

The coordinator of automation provides overall supervision of the data center and serves as the primary communication link between technical-services personnel and the systems department, a function that has expanded rather than diminished with time. She prepares informational and instructional documents for those using the technical-services system, alerts the systems department to operational problems, informs users of system changes and their effects on operations, and helps supervisors integrate the system into the workflow they manage. Although NOTIS frequently is used by staff in public services and in the branches, the coordinator is concerned mainly with facilitating the use of the system by technical-services personnel.

At the time of our study, there were about fifty cathode-ray terminals installed in the library for NOTIS use, with only about half within technical services. The others were in public-service departments and in branch libraries. Most of the public-service terminals were not installed until 1978. The delay reflects the library's concentration of resources, first on the development of a tool to support the activities of the circulation department, and then on a system to support the activities of the acquisitions and cataloging departments. After an extensive enhancement of the acquisitions and cataloging system was completed in 1977, resources allocated for the improvement of operations through automation were more widely cast to encompass public services.

Public-service librarians wanted to use NOTIS long before they were offered terminals. The data NOTIS houses are useful for item selection and reference activities and can be more conveniently retrieved with a terminal than by searching hardcopy files. In fact, much of NOTIS's data is not duplicated in hardcopy files. For example, the serials department ceased recording periodical holdings in the library's card catalogs when it began to enter the data in NOTIS.

When the revised acquisitions and cataloging system was unveiled in 1977, demand by public-service librarians for access to NOTIS became more fervent. The new system made much more flexible the way in which bibliographic records could be searched. Previously a search had been based on a key derived from an item's author and title. The new system included full author or title access, comparable to that which accompanies an author/title catalog. One could page through author and title indexes, the entries of which were linked to their corresponding bibliographic records. The former searching technique, based on derived keys, had not allowed one to browse through the contents of the bibliographic file. Furthermore, retrieving a record with only a limited knowledge of its associated title or author was awkward and often unsuccessful. The index access to NOTIS's bibliographic data relieved these problems.

As can be seen in figure 2-3, the public-services division is composed of eleven departments, all residing in the main library. Seven of the units are responsible for the maintenance of discrete and specialized collections. They appear in the right column of the public-services block. The remaining departments of public services are reference, circulation, interlibrary loan, and management services. In addition to carrying out its traditional responsibilities, the general-reference department administers the periodicals reading room. Management services is staffed by three librarians, who support the teaching programs of the Graduate School of Management through collection development and reference activities. The management collection is interfiled with the main collection.

The circulation department is, of course, responsible for the flow of materials in and out of the library. As has been previously suggested, the circulation function is laden with clerical tasks. At Northwestern, NOTIS accomplishes or helps in the accomplishment of many of these tasks. For example, it automatically generates overdue notices for items that have not been discharged by their due date. It also produces recall and find notices and notices that books are available. Throughout the main library are placed self-service check-out terminals that let library users charge books to their accounts without involving circulation-department personnel. Most charges are accomplished in this manner. Circulation-desk attendants spend their time processing recalled items and renewing or discharging materials, aided, of course, by NOTIS.

Machine-readable identification cards are enclosed in each circulating title. Data for NOTIS's circulation records are drawn from these cards. The information contained in the library's pool of identification cards is cumulated in an off-line file, providing Northwestern with a machine-readable list of its circulating titles. Each summer the list is poured onto paper, which is bound into volumes and stored behind the circulation desk. The volumes are often used by desk attendants to answer questions about holdings. However, the main function of the printed file is to support a periodic inventory of Northwestern's collections.

Except for those in the circulation department and in interlibrary loan, public-service librarians using NOTIS primarily call upon its technical-services system, searching the bibliographic data base in response to user questions about holdings or in support of their collection-development activities. The on-line circulation data can, of course, be used to determine the shelf status of titles. However, most library users who want to know whether titles are available for lending resolve their questions without librarian intervention. At the time of our study, a self-service cathode-ray terminal located near the public card catalog could be used for retrieving the desired information. Since our study, the library has introduced a public-access on-line catalog and has installed eleven more terminals for library users. The terminals can be used to search the catalog as well as the circulation data base.

In addition to its CRT for NOTIS use, the reference department maintains a printer terminal for the on-line search of and retrieval from the data bases of BRS, Lockheed, SDC, and *The New York Times*. The department has offered users access to machine-readable bibliographic data since 1974, when it provided free batch searches of the Educational Resources Information Center data base, (ERIC). Two years later it added on-line access to the Lockheed bases, passing on to users the Lockheed charges. Initially, the library administration thought the on-line service would fail. It was not convinced that users would pay for computerized data retrieval. However, demand was discovered, and through the years the reference department has expanded the service, adding the bases of other vendors. The reference department is the library's primary search site, although the transportation library and the science and engineering library also offer computerized data retrieval.

At the time of our study all branches of the library system except for the music library reported to the library director through an assistant university librarian. The music librarian, as can be seen in figure 2–3, reported directly. The science and engineering branch library administers two other branches, one in geology and another in mathematics. Each is located near the academic department it supports.

The music and the science and engineering branches use NOTIS's circulation system. They use the technical-services system also but primarily to support their reference and collection-development activities. The acquisition and cataloging of all scientific and technical material is handled by the technical-services division. In contrast, the music library depends on the technical-services departments for only part of its processing needs. It acquires some of its materials and does all of its cataloging. However, it does not input records into NOTIS. Instead it turns to data-center staff who enter the order and catalog records the music library generates. Generally, only staff from the technical-services division are allowed to enter or update NOTIS records. Furthermore, even within technical services, constraints are placed on who may create or modify records. The library administration has imposed these restrictions because it believes them necessary to insure the security and integrity of the data.

Northwestern's collection development is overseen by a collection-management division. Twenty-five librarians are assigned funds to purchase materials. Only five participate in collection development on a full-time basis. They are designated bibliographers. The rest share their collection development responsibilities with other public-service assignments. All report to the assistant university librarian for collection management on matters relating to collection development. Of the five bibliographers, four are formally assigned to the collection-management division. The other is a member of the Africana department.

A terminal is installed in the collection-management division to aid the division's bibliographers in their item-selection activities. It is primarily used by the division's clerical staff to ascertain whether contemplated acquisitions already have been ordered or acquired by the library. NOTIS is also relied on by item selectors in other departments to determine whether titles already have been ordered or acquired. NOTIS's fiscal support of collection development is limited. NOTIS monitors order records to track the amount of money committed and expended from each fund, and the resulting data are distributed to item selectors. However, it plays no role in the processing of invoices and payment of bills.

University of Washington

The Washington Library Network is directed by the Washington State Library in Olympia, and the Washington State Computing Center in Pullman hosts the network's computer system. The University of Washington in Seattle has played a part in the network's evolution. However, it has assumed a surprisingly small role in the system's development when one considers the importance of its libraries to the region. The University of Washington houses the largest collection in the Northwest, totaling some four-million volumes, and acquires over four times more in new material each year than do the other regional giants, the libraries of the Washington State University and the University of Oregon.

The University of Washington's small role is explained in part by the state library's early initiative in directing networklike services supported by computer systems. In 1966, the state library was one of sixteen libraries selected to participate in the MARC pilot project, an evaluation of the preliminary version of the MARC format. The state library used the MARC tapes to produce a union book catalog for the current acquisitions of three of the state's public library systems. WLN's computer system is really an outgrowth of this initial effort at using computer technology to facilitate interlibrary sharing of information and library resources.

The University of Washington library started using the network system in 1977 and became an OCLC member in 1978. The library's delay in joining a cooperative was due in part to a feeling of obligation to the state's emerging system, which was not operational until 1977. It was also due to the library administration's desire to monitor developments in computer-based library networking before making a commitment to join a bibliographic cooperative.

The library chose to participate in OCLC as well as WLN to compare the usefulness of the systems. In 1978, WLN's data base contained little more than MARC records. It is still considerably smaller than the data bases of the other cooperatives, RLG and OCLC, a situation attributable to the presence of few research libraries among its members. At the time of our study only about 30 percent of the records the University of Washington library sought were in the system. In contrast, on OCLC the "hit-rate" was 70 percent. As mentioned earlier, WLN maintains considerable quality control over its data base. Concomitant with this are some costs: cataloging on WLN takes more time, may require more compromise to a library's local practices, and is more expensive for each transaction than cataloging on OCLC. Finally, WLN is regional in scope. Records entering the system are available only to libraries in the Northwest. Because the University of Washington library is among the nations's top twenty research libraries, the administration feels that information about the library's holdings and the original cataloging it produces are of national interest.

The discussion that follows will detail how organizational units within the library are using WLN and OCLC. As can be seen in figure 2–4, the activities of budgeting, personnel, and library publications report in a staff capacity to the director of the University of Washington library. The collection-management block in the figure refers to a council of about fourteen persons. Most of the council members represent the interests of item selectors assigned related areas of responsibility. For example, the fine-arts council member represents architecture, art, drama, and music selectors. About fifty selectors are involved in the library's collection development, and council members are chosen from their ranks. All but one of the selectors are librarians. Most work in public-service units; however, some come from technical services.

Technical services at Washington includes the traditional units of acquisitions, cataloging, and serials. The serials division is responsible for all aspects of serials processing, including their acquisition, cataloging, receipt, and distribution. In addition, the division maintains in the main library a periodicals floor that houses the humanities and social-sciences periodicals for those academic departments not served by branch libraries.

The other units of technical services are bibliographic projects and the systems office. Bibliographic projects was created with the intention of having some of its staff available to accomplish special projects. For example, the library had some time ago switched from the Dewey to the LC system of classification. However, some of the titles previously cataloged under Dewey retained their original codes. One of the projects planned for the unit was the reclassification of the Dewey-coded reference titles. Another project planned for bibliographic projects was the conversion of the library's catalog data to a machine-readable format for a future on-line circulation system and catalog. At the time of our study, bibliographic projects had only recently been formed and had not yet undertaken any special tasks. Instead, it was totally immersed in a continuing responsibility—catalog maintenance—filing new records into the library's catalogs; changing existing records to accommodate changes in LC subject headings; updating existing records to reflect changes in holdings, such as the acquisition of additional copies; and withdrawing the records of discarded items.

During our site visit, both WLN and OCLC were being used to support a number of activities in technical services. Within acquisitions, their use was limited to searching the data bases for bibliographic data about titles to be ordered. Such data were needed to verify that the requested titles actually existed and to define uniquely the titles for book vendors. Such data were also used in some instances to direct a search of the library's catalog and on-order file for duplicate or variant editions of the titles. As mentioned in chapter 1, one of the functions of an acquisitions division is to prevent unwanted duplicates or variations.

Monograph-cataloging activities at Washington were distributed be-

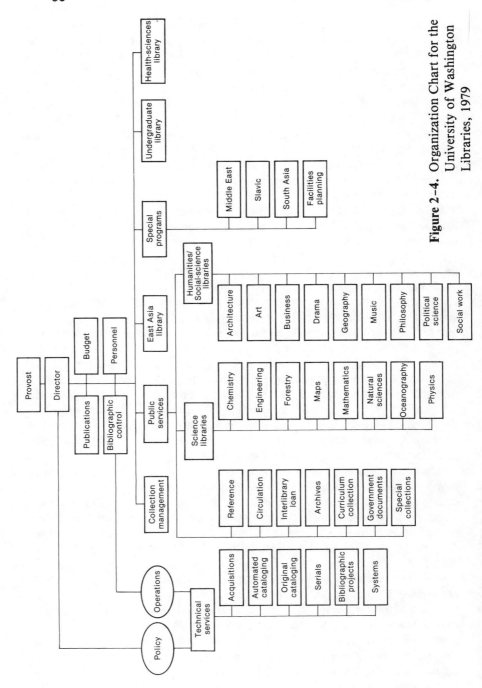

Figure 2-4. Organization Chart for the University of Washington Libraries, 1979

tween two divisions, automated and original cataloging. The use of WLN and OCLC was concentrated in automated cataloging. There, staff searched the data bases for catalog records created by other libraries. A subset of what was retrieved was used by Washington with minimal review. For the most part, the source of these records was LC. In fact, staff in automated cataloging would order catalog cards for records created by LC immediately upon their discovery.

Records created by libraries other than LC were reviewed and revised by staff in automated or original cataloging prior to card ordering, with librarians in original cataloging sent all records requiring the attention of a professional librarian. Original cataloging was also responsible for creating records for titles where no cataloging copy could be found by automated cataloging.

OCLC was the recipient of Washington's original cataloging. Staff in original cataloging were responsible for inputting the data into OCLC and requesting catalog cards. The use of WLN in original cataloging was limited to the authority file and searching for bibliographic data about Washington state and local documents. WLN maintained on-line those author and subject headings used by LC in their MARC records.

The serials division also was using WLN and OCLC, entering its original cataloging in both systems. In 1978, the library received a grant from the U.S. Office of Education to place full catalog records of all currently received serials into the WLN data base. The records were to include volumes held by the library, noting where in the library system volumes could be found.

Of the two systems, OCLC was being relied upon almost exclusively by the serials division to retrieve cataloging data and exclusively for catalog-card production. WLN maintained the MARC monograph and serials files on-line, but it did not offer the unauthenticated records from CONSER (Conservation of Serials), a cooperative serials cataloging project. Also, since WLN membership was primarily public libraries, little of the serials cataloging contributed by WLN users was of use to Washington. In addition to having the MARC monograph and serials files, OCLC had the unauthenticated CONSER records and the serials cataloging of numerous academic-library users. At the time of our study, Washington's serials division was finding catalog records for 60 percent of the titles it sought on OCLC.

As our discussion suggests, technical services was heavily involved in using both WLN and OCLC. However, the systems office played essentially no role in these activities. Systems involvement in the library's automation effort was for the most part limited to three activities. Systems staff keypunched, cumulated, and analyzed by computer circulation-related data. They were involved in the development of a management information system for the library. They were also involved in the maintenance of a machine-readable file of books on order and books awaiting cataloging. Periodically, microfiche copies of the file were distributed to item selectors and public-service units; and the acquisitions division received a daily print-out of the data, added since the last issue of the master file.

The In-Process File, as it was called, contained only about 80 percent of the titles actually in process. The file had been implemented in 1970, and changes in the mode of data entry and the batch programs that processed the data had lagged behind changes in the computer-center hardware and software; the outcome was difficulties in reading and manipulating the data. At the time of our study, the acquisitions division was considering various remedies to the problem of inaccurate in-process information.

Immediately before our study, the technical-services unit at the University of Washington library underwent a major restructuring. Previously, the divisions of technical services had reported to the library director through an associate director; and the staffs of bibliographic projects, automated cataloging, and original cataloging were part of a single unit, the cataloging division. As figure 2-4 reflects, reorganization resulted in splitting the cataloging activities. Furthermore, after the restructuring, technical-services-division heads no longer reported to an associate director. Instead, they reported to both the library director and the coordinator for bibliographic control. Policy matters were the concern of the director; day-to-day supervision of operations was the responsibility of the coordinator.

Generally, catalogers are more concerned with the accuracy and completeness of bibliographic data describing items and the integrity of systems for retrieving catalog records than with the speed with which titles are cataloged and made available to users. At Washington, the library director wanted to shift the concern of catalogers more toward favoring availability of materials. There was a level of cataloging that was unacceptable, but in the director's opinion, cataloging at Washington was already well above it. Experimentation was required to determine procedures that would result in minimizing cataloging time while simultaneously maintaining an acceptable level of cataloging. The director felt this experimentation could more readily take place if he became involved directly in technical-service operations.

The splitting of the cataloging function into several divisions further facilitated the needed experimentation. A common issue within a cataloging unit is the acceptability of the catalog records created by other institutions. Research libraries tend to conform to the procedures employed by LC. Thus, the records produced by LC are often accepted by research libraries with perhaps minor changes. In contrast, cataloging from institutions other than LC is treated more critically. Here there is usually more variation in the exact form of the subjects or authors selected to index the records. Call numbers acceptable at one library may be considered incomplete, inaccurate, or inappropriate at another.

Librarians working as original catalogers are by training sensitive to the quality of catalog records and the ease with which they can be integrated into the library's files. They often do not wish to borrow data from records produced elsewhere without careful scrutiny. Also, within cataloging, original catalogers tend to be most influential in determining cataloging procedures because the unit's librarians are concentrated in this group. At Washington, this combination of caution and influence was making it difficult for staff retrieving catalog records from the on-line data bases to experiment freely with different procedures. Granting these individuals divisional status increased their influence relative to original catalogers and allowed them to play a more active role in determining procedures.

At the time of our study, cataloging procedures were in a state of flux. In fact, according to personnel in both automated and original cataloging, procedures seemed to change daily. During our site visit, automated cataloging was experimenting with ordering cards for retrieved records before reviewing them for possible discrepancies between the cataloging practice of the Washington library and that of the library that created the record. They were also weighing the benefits of different levels of OCLC use relative to WLN system use.

Most branches of Washington's library system are part of public services. Exceptions are the health-sciences library, the undergraduate library, and the East Asia library. As can be seen in figure 2–4, the heads of these libraries report to the library director. Sixteen branch libraries reside within public services. Public services also includes a number of units housed in the main library: reference, circulation, interlibrary loan, curriculum materials, government documents, special collections, and archives and manuscripts.

The science branches within public services make up a science department. The remaining nine branches of public services form a social sciences/ humanities department. Branch librarians report to the associate director for public services through department supervisors. In contrast, divisions of the main library within public services report to the associate director.

The public-services units using automated support tools include branch libraries, the reference division, and the interlibrary-loan office. Five of the branches and the reference division offer computerized searches of the bibliographic data bases of SDC, Lockheed, and the *New York Times.* Their areas of responsibility correspond to their collection strengths. In addition, the health-sciences library offers searches of MEDLINE and other data bases maintained by the National Library of Medicine.

The health-sciences library began offering computerized bibliographic searching in the early 1970s. The reference division in the main library became involved in search services in 1973; however it was not until 1976 that an active program to publicize the service was undertaken and other branch libraries became service points. At the time of our study, library staff involved in searching met monthly to share information. A coordinator of on-line searching, located within the reference division, presided over the sessions and performed a number of administrative tasks associated with the service. However, the coordinator was not formally designated as a supervisor.

The only use of WLN in public services was in the main library's reference division, where, just prior to our study, WLN terminals had been installed. Reference used WLN primarily to search the library's serials data for the locations and call numbers of requested serials titles. Monographic titles held by the library and documented in WLN were too limited in number to make WLN a useful tool when answering questions on monographic holdings. The library intended to offer users subject searches of the bibliographic records in WLN, producing printouts of the resulting bibliographies. The administrative details of this service—in particular, its cost to users—were being worked out during our site visit.

OCLC's only user within public services was the interlibrary-loan office. At the time of our study, the office was evaluating OCLC's recently implemented interlibrary-loan system. Because records in OCLC include libraries holding the titles, OCLC has always been used by its members to identify potential lenders. The OCLC interlibrary-loan system added another dimension to this support by providing a mechanism by which libraries could both communicate borrowing needs and respond to requests.

At the time of our study, the interlibrary-loan office did not use WLN to find locations in the Northwest from which material could be borrowed. The office had a more comprehensive guide to regional holdings right outside its door—the Pacific Northwest Bibliographic Center (PNBC) catalog. The PNBC was established in the 1940s to facilitate interlibrary loans among libraries in the Northwest. Its primary responsibility was the maintenance of a union catalog of the holdings of some fifty regional libraries. Since our study of Washington, the PNBC catalog has been closed, a casualty of library automation. Its major users were participating in OCLC, WLN, or UTLAS (University of Toronto Library Automation System), a Canadian-based cooperative, making the cost of the location service provided by PNBC's catalog difficult to justify.

An associate director supervises the library unit called *Special Programs,* pictured in figure 2–4 as the last major group of blocks. Three area-studies programs are part of special programs, covering the Middle East, South Asia, and the Slavic countries. Before the reorganization of technical services, area-program staff were distributed between the acquisitions and cataloging divisions. Within Special Programs, they continue their prior activities—collection development, reference, and technical processing.

However, it is intended that their involvement in the last activity will decrease relative to their involvement in collection development and reference. Also within Special Programs is facilities planning and management, which is concerned with the development of new space, maintenance of existing space, and long-range planning for the physical plant.

Summary

When the libraries of Chicago, Stanford, and Northwestern began their automation projects in the mid-1960s, automation in libraries meant off-line support for narrowly defined tasks; for example, an in-process file maintained by batch runs, with file data periodically printed and copied for the several library units who made use of it. Computer centers did not yet operate as providers of general services, nor were they preceived as such. Furthermore, computer centers were not as user-oriented as they are now. In fact, higher-level computer-programming languages were in their infancy. Cathode-ray terminals were not yet available, and the experimental time-sharing systems of the day relied upon noisy and intolerably slow typewriter-terminals. Operating systems were unreliable and inadequate for the kind of support each of the libraries desired.

All three libraries wanted to develop *integrated* library systems. They wanted a single system that would serve the library as a whole—rather than numerous systems each supporting the specific needs of an isolated function. All three libraries eventually settled into the development of systems built around machine-readable data bases accessible to all library units in real-time through terminal links. The ultimate promise of such systems was the elimination of the numerous, cumbersome, and often overlapping paper files that crowded libraries, and the elimination of the tremendous amount of duplication in effort that was required for their maintenance.

Stanford was the first to tackle the major obstacle blocking the development of on-line, file-based library systems, the software needed to support the creation, update, and use of large files of data. The Stanford library was tremendously aided in this task by the SPIRES project. Indeed, without it BALLOTS's first generation might have looked more like the batch-oriented book-processing system that Chicago initially developed.

The Stanford and Chicago projects did not proceed with each library unaware of the progress of the other. Considerable interaction occurred between the project staffs. In fact, in 1968 the Chicago, Stanford, and Columbia libraries received support from the National Science Foundation (NSF) to develop and evaluate a strategy by which the sites could collaborate in their efforts to build computer-based library tools. Numerous meetings were called during this project's tenure, among them two major conferences in which developments were reported to participants from the general library community. The major outcome of the NSF project, though, was the conclusion that formal collaboration was not possible. In particular, the project concluded that implementing a single system that a number of libraries would use was fraught with difficulties. Paul Fasana has described many of the obstacles the libraries of Chicago, Stanford, and Columbia encountered.[2] When the NSF project ended in mid-1969, the three libraries essentially went their separate ways. However, each continued to keep abreast of the progress of the others through informal contacts.

Northwestern's development project started later than those at Stanford and Chicago. In fact, by the time Northwestern was ready to seek external support for the implementation of computer-based tools, public and private funding agencies were no longer interested in supporting local library projects. Awards had already been made to a number of libraries, including the major undertakings of Stanford, Chicago, and Columbia. There was little to justify the spending of more public or private funds on still another demonstration of the application of computers in libraries.

When compared to the LDMS and BALLOTS, some fundamental differences in NOTIS are apparent, differences that can be attributed to the reliance on internal support for its development. Both Chicago and Stanford chose to accomplish and, through contractual agreements with their funding agents, were committed to accomplish more than the building of systems to support their local operations. Government and private funding agencies would not have granted monies to projects with such a narrow focus. Rather, both institutions undertook projects that were justified on the basis of their contributions to the library community more generally.

The Northwestern library, in contrast, focused more closely on the needs of its organization and user community. Indeed, it was compelled to do so to justify the spending of university monies on NOTIS's development. The funds at its disposal were not intended for basic research.

The cost of developing and operating each module of NOTIS was considerably more visible to the library and its funding agent, the university, than was the case at Chicago and Stanford. The allocation of funds for NOTIS's development and operation followed the university's normal budgeting process. Monies were received on a year-to-year basis to finance specified components of NOTIS. After a component was implemented, the cost of its operation was included as an item in subsequent library budgets.

Both Chicago and Stanford worked with federal-agency grants that supported several years of effort. Numerous project activities proceeded in parallel, with resources allocated to development often difficult to separate from those allocated to system operation and maintenance. It was really only during periods in which external grant funding ebbed that the Chicago and Stanford libraries could effectively distinguish between the development and operating costs of their systems.

Because the acquisitions and cataloging functions generate and maintain the data in the central and most important library file, the public catalog, it is logical to begin the development of an integrated library system within technical services.

Chicago and Stanford began their automation activities within technical services. Northwestern, on the other hand, elected to begin with circulation. The decision to start with circulation was in large part a result of Northwestern's dependence upon university funds. Circulation is a highly visible function, an activity that users can observe directly. In contrast, the activities of acquisitions and cataloging are invisible to users. Northwestern's library administration believed that future funding for NOTIS would be more likely if the library began its venture with a system component that allowed users, and in particular, faculty users to experience directly the advantages of an automated library.

After the libraries of Chicago, Stanford, and Northwestern had more or less settled into the local operation of their systems, each began to consider further avenues of development. A fundamental difference emerged in the routes they selected. Both Chicago and Northwestern stressed the importance of support for the entire range of library functions through the development of linked local and regional systems, tied to still another system gathering and maintaining bibliographic data on a national level. Stanford opted for the development of a centrally located system. That system would serve geographically dispersed libraries, with the range of centrally supported services limited to functions within which generalized systems would be both acceptable to users and efficient to operate through long-distance communications.

Shortly after our field visit, Chicago began working with the University of Wisconsin and the IBM Corporation to develop a system that would distribute library functions and data between a centrally located mainframe computer and locally maintained minicomputers. Also shortly after our study, Northwestern joined RLG. However, it is still operating NOTIS, and, in fact, is marketing the system to other libraries. Stanford, of course, continues to play a key role in the evolution of the nationwide system for which it is largely responsible, RLIN.

Because of its relative lack of experience in the area of library automation, the University of Washington library provided a fascinating contrast to the libraries of Chicago, Stanford and Northwestern. It was just beginning the move toward a major commitment to automation. At the time of our visit, Washington was experimenting with the use of WLN and OCLC and planning for the implementation of a circulation system and an on-line catalog.

Until 1978, the library's involvement in automation had been limited to the development and operation of several narrowly focused batch-processing systems. It participated in WLN policy-setting committees, but it was not a key actor in WLN's system development. In fact, the Washington library has chosen to limit its participation in WLN to maintaining its serials record on-line and to resource sharing. Original cataloging of monographs is entered into the OCLC system, which also receives its serials cataloging.

In addition to experience with automation, the four libraries varied on other notable dimensions, including the source of their funding for computer-based tools, the control they had over the systems they were using, the stability of their operations, and the access they had to bibliographic data originating from other libraries. The variation in the sources of their funding has been mentioned earlier as contributing to some fundamental differences between NOTIS and the two systems developed with considerable outside aid—the LDMS and BALLOTS/RLIN. At the time of our study, Chicago's external support had ceased. Money for the enhancement, operation, and maintenance of the LDMS was at that time coming entirely from university allocations. Northwestern was supporting its system in the manner in which it had always done; that is, through its allocations from the university. Both sites were introducing system enhancements and planning on future enhancements. However, the Chicago library appeared considerably more uncertain about the viability of its development program. It now had to depend on university funds, a mode of support for the LDMS with which the library had relatively little experience. Norhtwestern, in contrast, was comfortable with the requisite campus politics and more certain of continuing support.

The University of Washington library was depending on university monies to support its network memberships and future system implementations. In fact, it had just submitted a request to the university for funds to automate circulation and develop an on-line catalog. The library intended to supplement university funds whenever possible with outside support. Indeed, all four libraries sought external support for projects that would not only help them reach their ultimate automation goals but would also be of value to the library community. The U.S. Office of Education project to upgrade on the WLN data-base records for Washington's currently received serials is an example of just such an undertaking. For Washington, the project's outcome was an important step toward the creation of a machine-readable file of complete cataloging records and holdings for its serials.

When we visited Stanford, the university was still receiving much external support for the development of RLIN, but now as a member of RLG rather than as a direct recipient of the grants. The power to direct the spending of these funds was shared by Stanford and the other RLG members, a great dilution of the control Stanford had exerted over its system before it was acquired by RLG. The movement of RLIN/BALLOTS out of the realm of the library's full control actually began in the early 1970s, when

BALLOTS was placed under the jurisdiction of the computer center. It continued when the BALLOTS network was implemented in the mid-1970s and the computer center had to respond to the requirements of other users. However, at that point in BALLOTS's networking, the priorities of the Stanford library still reigned well above those of other libraries. When RLG acquired BALLOTS, Stanford's control diminished considerably; the priorities of other network users, in particular the RLG members, assumed equal importance.

The University of Washington, as a network user rather than a network owner, had still less control over its major tools, OCLC and WLN, than Stanford did over its computer-based tools. As system owners, Northwestern and Chicago were at the other extreme with essentially complete control over their systems.

During our investigation, change within the organizations was most extreme at Washington, where major operational and structural alterations were occurring simultaneously. The library was attempting to streamline its technical processing by incorporating computer-based tools. At the same time, it was redesigning the organization responsible for technical processing. Stanford was also undergoing notable change, learning how to cope with instability in RLIN services and operation as the system moved toward multi-research-library support, redefining its relationship with RLIN personnel, and responding to the requirements of membership in a new organization, RLG. In contrast to Washington and Stanford, Northwestern and Chicago were stable settings, although Chicago was experiencing some turbulence as a consequence of losing external support for its system.

Finally, the institutions varied in the access they had to cataloging data originating from other libraries. Washington's access was most extensive. Through OCLC it could search the MARC data, the serials records created through project CONSER, and the original cataloging contributed by OCLC's membership, which in mid-1979 stood at over one thousand libraries. RLIN's data base at the time contained little more than MARC records and the cataloging that had been entered by the Stanford libraries. The system had been able only recently to accommodate the cataloging of the Columbia University library and was still unable to support the processing of other RLG members. Total RLG membership at the time of our study was eight.

Northwestern and Chicago had machine access to MARC data and their own cataloging, but little else. Through the *National Union Catalog,* cataloging data originating from numerous sources were flowing into their organizations. However, these volumes were undoubtedly much more awkward to search than machine-readable files and provided more limited coverage than available through OCLC and anticipated through RLIN.

Notes

1. Joel Shurkin, "The Rise and Fall and Rise of RLG," pp. 450–455.
2. Paul J. Fasana, "The Collaborative Library Systems Development Project." For the interested reader, this volume also contains a brief description of Columbia's early efforts in automation.

3   Structure

All complex organizations, including academic libraries, assign tasks to individuals, the accomplishment of which contributes to the achievement of organizational goals. For example, in a library one individual catalogs materials in the romance languages, another answers questions at the reference desk in the undergraduate library, and a third discharges returned materials. The process of delegating tasks is referred to as the *division of labor*. Usually, the specific tasks assigned to an individual are specified formally in a job description. These descriptions are used in matching qualified individuals with positions and in assessing job performance. Most university libraries have job descriptions for all full-time and many of their part-time positions.

To insure that the sum of individual task accomplishments in the division of labor results in overall goal attainment, two additional aspects of organizational structure are necessary, the table of organization and the distribution of authority. Individual task assignments that are similar or interrelated are grouped, giving rise to the formation of units, often called sections, departments, or divisions. For example, individuals involved in ordering and monitoring the delivery of monographs are assigned to an acquisitions department. In larger organizations, there are higher-level groupings of similar or complementary departments to form divisions. In some instances, these higher-level groupings may include units with similar attributes, such as branch libraries. In other instances, grouping may be based upon the nature of tasks accomplished; for example, acquisitions, cataloging, and serials are frequently collected in a technical-services division. This aspect of organizational structure, known as the *table of organization,* is usually portrayed in the organization chart.

In addition to a division of labor and a table of organization, the other general feature needed to insure goal attainment is a system for distributing authority. This system is also known as the *supervisory structure,* which insures that all individuals and units complete their assigned tasks in the prescribed manner and, frequently, within predetermined time schedules. It coordinates the flow of resources, products, services, and information among various internal units and between the organization and its environment. In academic libraries, for example, we have such diverse positions as supervisor of the original cataloging unit, chief of the serials department, assistant director for public services, and head of the development office.

Today, it is a very rare complex organization that exists in a stable environment. As mentioned above, academic libraries are now among the most rapidly changing organizations, and automation is a major contributor to constantly fluctuating conditions. In this chapter we first describe and analyze changes in the division of labor and table of organization that have accompanied the introduction of computer-aided systems in our case-study libraries. Our discussion will be organized by the functional areas introduced in chapter 1: collection management, acquisitions, cataloging, circulation, and reference services. The sections on acquisitions and cataloging deal primarily with the processing of books. Because of the unique problems associated with the processing of serials, their acquisition and cataloging are treated separately. The chapter continues with a discussion of the systems function and concludes with a brief analysis of the changing nature of the authority or supervisory structure in university libraries.

Collection Management

The goal of the collection-management function is to insure that the materials needed by library users are available through library services. The needs of both present and future users are considered. Those associated with collection development identify publications the library should acquire and submit requests for their order to acquisitions staff. Increasingly, their decisions are mediated by the holdings of other libraries with whom inter-library-sharing agreements are established. Figure 3–1 summarizes the major relationships influencing collection development.

The identification of publications involves surveying numerous sources that vary tremendously in the usefulness of the information they provide about publications, the timeliness of the data, and the comprehensiveness with which they cover the range of publications they are most concerned with. Sources include Library of Congress catalog records, national and subject bibliographies, the advertisements and catalogs of publishers, and booklists and reviews in library and scholarly journals.

The identification of user needs relies on formal and informal contacts with users and awareness of the kinds of topics covered in current publications. Increasingly, selectors have access to circulation data that quantify the use of different parts of the collection. All of the above methods to assess needs provide more reliable estimates of present than of future needs. Librarians have developed few ways to infer future requirements.[1]

How systematic those in collection development are in identifying possible acquisitions and user needs varies across selectors, a function

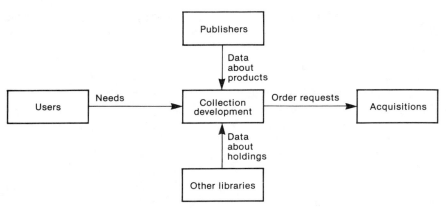

Figure 3-1. Collection Development

primarily of the priority of collection development relative to other responsibilities and of the ease with which relevant information is available. Bibliographers, who as a rule are full-time collection developers, tend to be
exhaustive in their search for acquisitions. Faculty responsible for item
selection tend to rely on the scholarly journals they regularly read and
publishers' advertisements.[2]

The computer-based tools that support collection developments are
limited in the range of tasks they aid. For the most part, the tools are components of technical-services systems that have been adapted for use in or
are supplying data of value to collection development. Their application has
not significantly altered procedures or the set of tasks traditionally associated with the function of collection development.

At the libraries we visited, the computer-based tools being used by
collection-development personnel were among the most sophisticated systems available to aid in the identification of possible acquisitions and the
analysis of library holdings. They are, of course, systems that allow access
to the MARC tapes and to the machine-readable catalog records of local
holdings as well as those of other libraries. The analysis of user needs was
not being helped by computer-based tools. Two of the sites, Chicago and
Northwestern, had automated circulation systems and thus the potential to
generate considerable information about past and present use. Both systems, for example, stored historical data on circulating titles, data that
could be used for such things as selecting titles for remote storage. However, neither site had yet fully exploited the potential of their systems to aid
collection-development tasks.

Those item selectors with access to MARC data used it most often as a
means to identify titles that had not come to their attention through the

printed sources they also monitored. Most titles appropriate for acquisition were ordered long before their appearance in MARC tapes. More timely machine-readable data bases of new publications are available but have not yet been exploited to aid item selection. For example, several major book jobbers maintain data bases of their inventories. Also, machine-readable lists of new publications are becoming more readily available as a by-product of computer-aided printing of new review journals.

Many item selectors interviewed during the course of the case studies spoke enthusiastically about computer-based tools in libraries. However, they also recounted their frustrations with automated systems as they currently exist. Perhaps the most common problem was gaining access to a terminal. Item selectors tend to be located in public-service units. At the time of our study, few terminals were distributed among these units. Also, many selectors had little faith in the reliability of automated acquisitions systems, although most recognized that problems were more often caused by data-entry personnel than by a malfunctioning of the software or computer. It was a common practice for item selectors to maintain manual order files as a backup to the on-line data maintained by acquisitions departments.

Some item selectors found that the specificity required by automated systems did not correspond with their normal operating procedures. For example, item selectors often order titles from prepublication lists. By the time such materials arrive their titles are frequently different from those previously announced. When acquisitions staff attempt to retrieve order records for these titles, no records are found, and the processing of the material is delayed by a considerable amount of unproductive activity. Such title changes also produce many dead records in the data base. Furthermore, numerous invalid claims are generated from the initially entered records for which no book or serial bearing the earlier titles exists.

As more item selectors have access to on-line data and as more sources describing new publications become available for on-line browsing, we may anticipate considerable change in the process of collection development. There is no question that monitoring a machine-readable data base of new publications is more effective than physically leafing through numerous printed sources. It is also more efficient and perhaps will encourage item selectors not now comprehensively surveying new material in their areas of concern to improve their coverage. The distinction between item selection and acquisition will become less clear as data bases improve and become more accessible. The process of submitting an order for acquisition and ordering the title from a vendor becomes indistinguishable, if the system can be relied upon to supply the necessary bibliographic data and to perform a preorder check of holdings. Finally, improvement in on-line access to the holdings of other libraries will prompt the evolution of more active programs for sharing acquisitions. More interlibrary sharing is already occurring among the RLG libraries. The distance that once discouraged the sharing of material among these research libraries is being bridged by the real-time communication system that now connects them.

Acquisitions

As mentioned in chapter 1, acquisitions involves all the clerical tasks of placing an order, insuring timely and accurate delivery, and accomplishing appropriate fund accounting. Figure 3-2 schematically portrays the acquisitions process. Collection development, that body of activities leading to item selection, results in the passing of order requests to the acquisitions department. Preorder searching gathers sufficient data to identify items uniquely and determine whether they or variations of them (for example, translations) are already in the collection or on order. If not, purchase orders are generated and submitted to appropriate suppliers. The acquisitions staff then monitors delivery of the ordered materials. If an item is not received by a predetermined date, a claim to the supplier is initiated. Upon receipt of an item, it is examined to insure a correspondence between the purchase order and what has been received. If the material is correct, procedures are activated to pay the supplier, and the item is forwarded to the cataloging department.

As depicted in figure 3-2, the acquisitions process is fairly simple and straightforward. However, in large university libraries tens of thousands of orders are processed each year. For example, in 1977–1978 Stanford ordered over thirty-nine thousand titles. Although acquisitions is not a complex process, it is complicated by the volume of order requests flowing in from collection development and by the number of purchase orders as yet unfilled. It is a most appropriate candidate for computer-aided support.

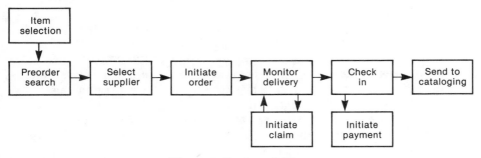

Figure 3-2. Acquisitions

Automation is promoting changes in task assignments and the division of labor in acquisition departments. For example, preorder searches for bibliographic data increasingly uncover machine-readable records from the MARC tapes or from the OCLC or RLIN files. These records can be read directly into an acquisitions file to form an order record. Consequently, preorder search activities are increasingly producing the on-line record that subsequently is used to generate a purchase order. The Stanford acquisitions department's search and order activities were recently reorganized into one unit, a demonstration of the closer liaison between those operations fostered by automation.

Another change in task assignment accompanying automation affects claims units. In manual systems, clerical personnel must leaf through order files to identify delinquent items. They also must type and mail the necessary claim notices. Computer-supported acquisitions systems can automatically complete daily searches of the on-line order file and print lists of delinquent items for review by acquisitions staff. Such systems can also be instructed to print claims notices in a format ready for mailing to suppliers. Thus the need for a large clerical staff in claims units is greatly diminished.

A common feature of automated acquisitions systems is their centralization in a machine-readable file of information on materials-in-process. This feature is found in both modular and integrated systems regardless of whether they are developed locally, commercially, or by utilities. Orders are initiated by creating new records that then enter a data file of items intended to become part of the library's collection. Changes may subsequently be made to order records to complete, correct, or update them. The order status of a title is often part of this record, charting the title's course before it reaches the library and as it progresses through technical services. Automated systems vastly increase the efficiency and speed with which items can be processed. However, a major problem is created by the dependence of technical-processing activities on the continuous and error-free functioning of the system and can be especially problematic when the system is designed for on-line use and the library shares a computing facility with other campus units.

For example, at the time of our study, the LDMS at Chicago operated on the central university computer, which also accommodated all research and instructional computing. User demand on university computing centers tends to peak at the end of grading periods, response time increases, and malfunctioning is more frequent. The library must have a continuous and relatively constant level of computing capacity. When the computer is overloaded and breakdowns occur, operating units of the library are affected differentially. Reference units can readily shift to a manual mode of operation, and circulation units can record transactions for later input to the system. However, activities in technical-services units, and particularly automated acquisitions, essentially come to a halt with computer-system failure. At the University of Chicago, staff in acquisitions reported that the LDMS averaged approximately 20 percent downtime during normal working hours. Not only did the failure undermine productivity, it was also most frustrating.

University libraries often entertain substantial gift programs. Gifts are donated by alumni, friends of the library, and others who wish to make their private collections more generally available. The gifts, of course, arrive in acquisitions departments as unordered items. Staff sort through the materials and usually consult with item selectors to determine which items should be added to the collection. Titles thought to be of tangential value are discarded.

On-line acquisitions systems have greatly aided the management of gift programs. First, they allow gift items to be represented more quickly in on-order files, blocking any new orders that would duplicate the materials. Chicago, for example, enters gift items in its on-order file even before the titles are routed to item selectors for decisions concerning their retention. Numerous features of the LDMS insure that the records are available to order librarians more quickly than they would have been under the manual system, including the system's editing support of record creation, its automatic filing of records, and the on-line availability of a substantial portion of the name and subject headings used by the library. The latter decreases the need to leaf through paper files for appropriate author entries to attach to the records.

The process of deciding whether gifts should be retained is also aided by on-line acquisitions systems, and aided even further when on-line cataloging systems are also available. Essential information in the decision to retain an item is its relationship to the collection. On-order files may have to be scrutinized, as well as the public catalog, the serials record, and files of cataloging backlogs. When these files, or even parts of them, are on-line, they can often be searched more efficiently. They can also be searched more effectively because automated systems usually provide more access points than are available with manual files.

Branch librarians are intimately involved in acquisitions activities. They are responsible for developing the branch collection, often with the assistance of faculty served by the branches. Branch librarians usually transmit their order requests to the acquisitions department in written form, for it is still unusual to have terminals distributed among the branches. For the most part, branch librarians resent not yet having terminals. They feel ignored and "out in the sticks" with respect to automation. In their view, technical processing for the collections of the main library may have improved, but library automation has had very little effect on the processing of branch materials. Most branch librarians report that they still maintain their manual files of pending orders, some because they have no terminal and thus no convenient way to review the on-line file, some because they have no faith that their orders will appropriately be entered into and monitored by the automated system.

Many of the branch librarians we interviewed at the sites with on-line technical-services systems indicated a change in the way they determined the status of ordered items. They previously had directed these queries to the clerical staff in acquisitions, but now they tended to get this information from reference librarians. Terminals in acquisitions are usually heavily scheduled for searching and ordering activities, and it is difficult to interrupt these operations to query the data base about whether an item has arrived or has been cataloged. On the other hand, terminals in reference are in use only when the user's request is being pursued; otherwise they tend to be idle. Consequently, reference librarians are increasingly providing assistance to their colleagues on technical-service inquiries.

University libraries as a rule do not issue payment for the materials they purchase, but work through the offices of the university comptroller. This lack of complete control over the movement of funds to vendors is a major obstacle in building automated accounting systems. In fact, none of our case-study libraries had fully automated the fiscal component of acquisitions, despite the sophistication of some of their systems. At Northwestern, for example, NOTIS monitored commitments against book funds, issuing a monthly statement of expenditures and encumbrances broken down by fund. However, bookkeepers processed invoices without the aid of the system, eventually routing them to the university comptroller.

In university libraries there are often selectors who bypass acquisitions units, acquiring material directly—another obstacle in designing automated accounting systems. For example, the Africana studies program at Northwestern spends thousands of dollars on materials that do not enter the acquisitions system. Thus the monthly statements generated by NOTIS often do not reflect accurately the spending activity of the Africana selectors.

At the end of the Stanford profile we commented on the overlap in the activities of item selectors and acquisitions staff. The responsibility for searching to insure against unwanted duplication is ultimately that of the acquisitions department. However, item selectors frequently search library files before submitting orders, their efforts often being repeated by those in acquisitions. At the end of the last section, we suggested that automated systems may lead to the complete assumption by item selectors of the responsibility for searching library files and even generating orders for submission to vendors. This assignment of responsibility would eliminate a considerable amount of wasted time—searching files that have already been searched, retrieving data that have already been retrieved, reformatting records that could have been placed into correct form by their original creators.

Some evidence exists that institutions are moving toward this reorganization of the acquisitions function. At Stanford, as we have already noted, a third of the on-line order file was input directly by item selectors, who were also responsible for the necessary preorder searching. We also noted another change at Stanford in acquisitions associated with automated systems—its participation in cataloging. In fact, Stanford's acquisitions department actually cataloged a subset of the library's new titles. More generally, acquisitions departments in institutions with automated technical-services systems are assuming tasks previously accomplished by cataloging units; for example, the tasks of searching for and retrieving catalog copy. Revising copy and original cataloging are still the responsibility of cataloging units.

Cataloging

Figure 3-3 is a representation of monographic cataloging in university libraries. As depicted, monographs are passed from the acquisitions department to a distribution unit. This unit in turn routes them to either the copy cataloging unit, the original cataloging unit, or the wait collection. If LC copy is available for a monograph, it is passed on to the copy-cataloging unit. If LC copy is not available, the book is passed on to the original-cataloging unit or placed in a waiting-for-cataloging collection. The decision to place a book in the wait collection is based on the expectation that it will be cataloged by LC eventually. If no LC cataloging can be expected, it is assigned to a professional librarian for original cataloging. In actual practice, many items without LC copy are routed to original cataloging despite their probable cataloging by LC; for example, reference works that quickly become dated or are frequently used may be treated in this way.

Items are removed from the wait collection when LC copy becomes available or when their access is requested by a library user. In the former instance, the items are sent to copy cataloging; in the latter, they are sent to original cataloging. When their cataloging is completed, the books are forwarded to end processing. As we mentioned in chapter 1, end processing involves a series of clerical steps such as placing call numbers on the spines of volumes and entering selected bibliographic information within the pages. Pockets for circulation cards and any necessary security devices are also inserted in end processing. After these tasks are completed, the volumes are forwarded to circulation for shelving and become available to users.

The most significant effect of automation on cataloging to date has

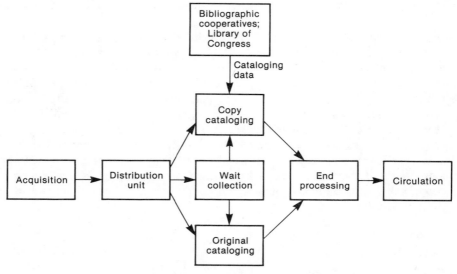

Figure 3-3. Cataloging

been in the area of copy cataloging. Automation has thus far had little effect on the activities of original catalogers. Our investigation uncovered no evidence of automation's having yet reduced the need for original cataloging in university libraries. Among our institutions, there were fewer original catalogers than there had been a decade before. However, the reason for the reduction was not a decrease in the need for original cataloging. Rather it was due to decreases in library budgets and greater emphasis upon copy cataloging.

Automation has resulted in an important organizational change in cataloging departments. Copy cataloging is usually performed by highly trained but nonetheless nonprofessional staff. Before automation, copy catalogers tended to report to original catalogers. In automated departments they tend to be grouped apart in units often of comparable stature to those occupied by original catalogers.

In our field work, we interviewed original catalogers who thought that they had lost status because of the changes brought by automated systems. The organizational shift of copy catalogers out of their sphere of supervision undoubtedly contributed to this perception. Also contributing to the perception of lost status was the relatively small role original catalogers had played in the implementation of automated systems. Copy catalogers were among the first in cataloging divisions to be exposed to the on-line systems; they received special training and much personal attention from immediate supervisors and, indeed, from the library administration more generally.

Copy catalogers interviewed in the course of our field work did not see themselves as having achieved any improvement of status. Rather, most of them thought they were performing a fairly routine clerical operation with the assistance of a computer system. They were still acutely aware that original catalogers were far more knowledgeable than they were about cataloging and indeed still sought their advice on cataloging matters. Hence, although the professional librarians perceived a loss in their own status, the loss was not compensated by an increase in status as perceived by copy catalogers.

The loss of perceived status among original catalogers is analogous to the recent decrease in perceived status among bibliographers in university libraries. During the 1950s and 1960s, university libraries enjoyed the luxury of what then appeared as unlimited financial support for expanding their collections. Many university libraries employed a large staff of bibliographers, assigned responsibility for obtaining both current and retrospective materials primarily for the main library. This staff frequently had earned advanced degrees in scholarly pursuits and were specialists in identifying and obtaining materials in their areas of expertise. Many also had part-time faculty appointments.

During the 1970s, the fiscal picture for university libraries, as well as for all institutions of higher education, changed dramatically. Budget cuts severely restricted funds for total expenditures in university libraries, and the effect of inflation and the declining value of the dollar further diminished the purchasing power of the shrinking budgets. University libraries had to cut their staffs of bibliographers and substantially trim their book funds. No longer are bibliographers permitted to fly off to exotic places on book-buying trips. Because communication is indirect and less frequent, international networks of book dealers, jobbers, and suppliers once nurtured by bibliographers have fallen into disrepair. And because of the decreased volume of new acquisitions, bibliographers interact less frequently with faculty. These changes have made bibliographers acutely sensitive to their status in the library and the university community at large, a status, so they believe, that has plummeted dramatically.

Cataloging arrears have plagued manual cataloging systems. University libraries have experienced arrears of several-hundred-thousand volumes. An important motivation for implementing automated systems has been the prospect of eliminating tremendous backlogs. In manual cataloging systems, the emphasis is usually placed on correct and complete processing of each individual item, but automated systems tend to place greater emphasis on an even and timely flow of materials. The increasing reliance of university libraries on machine-readable cataloging data created by LC and other libraries is still resisted by many original catalogers, who take pride in the accuracy of bibliographic information; for example, call numbers and subject headings that correspond to their perceptions of the unique needs of their user communities. Catalogers believe that the new emphasis on flow results in insufficient attention to individual items and in compromises to the accuracy and completeness of cataloging data.

An essential tool in a cataloging department is the *authority file,* which specifies the precise wording and punctuation that should be used for catalog-card entries. If a library has *established* an entry, a record will appear in the file specifying the accepted form and when it was adopted, forms previously used by the library, and variant forms; that is, forms that deviate from accepted forms but might be employed by public catalog users to retrieve the same records. For example, an authority record might list as the established form *Samuel Clemens* and list as a variant form *Mark Twain.* The primary function of an authority file is to insure that the entries of cards filed in the public catalog are consistent. Inconsistency complicates the task of locating all records of possible interest to the catalog user. In fact, inconsistency without cross-referencing makes it virtually impossible for the catalog user to be certain a search is complete.

Authority files include authors, titles of series, and uniform titles; that is, titles of works that may be referred to in different ways. The classic example of the latter is the Bible. Should this publication be called the *Holy Bible* or the *Holy Scriptures?* Subject headings would also be included in university authority files were it not for the Library of Congress, which publishes and frequently updates the subject headings it has established. University libraries generally rely on these volumes, manually appending subject headings employed locally that deviate from LC entries or have not yet been established by LC.

Variant forms of entry are filed in authority files to direct the catalogers to established forms through *see* cross-references. They also appear as entries in the public catalog to alert the catalog user that the records he or she seeks may be filed, but under a different entry. Thus in an attempt to retrieve records under *political theory,* a catalog user will be directed to *see political science. See also* cross-references are used in public catalogs to link related established entries or previously used forms that have been superseded.

Authority files are dynamic stores of information. New records are frequently added, old records are frequently revised. Many publications, for example, are authored by organizations such as the Technical Information Library at Bell Telephone or the American Society for Training and Development. Organizations frequently change their names. Thus new publications often arrive with their authors documented in the authority file, but under different names. The authority file must be updated to record such changes.

At the time of our study, all of the case-study sites were relying on manual authority files. The University of Washington through WLN had access to an on-line authority file based on the names, titles, and subjects that indexed WLN bibliographic records. The library's cataloging units made use of this file but also depended on locally maintained sources. All of the case-study libraries were planning for a future of on-line authority, either through cooperative or locally developed files. In fact, the Library of Congress had already issued a format for authority records, paving the way for interinstitutional sharing of authority records. In 1977, LC began releasing machine-readable tapes of its established subject headings through the MARC distribution service. Name authority records, including uniform titles, followed in 1978.

On-line authority files can ease the task of retrieving established entries, and updating, creating, and filing records. For example, catalogers can be provided with more ways to locate established forms, including, for example, keywords. Furthermore, if a variant form is used the computer can immediately display the appropriate authority data. With manual files, a cataloger must first locate the variant-entry card, find out from it what the established form is, and then search for the established-entry card.

The linking of an authority file to on-line bibliographic records, leading to what is called authority control, provides still more aid for cataloging. The computer can be relied on to alert a cataloger that the entries of newly filed records deviate from previously used entries. This automatic checking would eliminate clerical errors in names and subjects. With manual catalogs, when LC changes a subject heading all cards affected by the change must be pulled, revised, and refiled if consistency with LC is desired. With automated authority control, a single transaction affects an entry change immediately on all records in which the older term appears.

Catalog maintenance is concerned primarily with filing new cards and revising old cards in the public catalog and removing obsolete cards. It is a burdensome and time-consuming activity. Accuracy is essential because a misfiled card is essentially a lost record. Catalog-maintenance units must be staffed with individuals well trained in filing rules. They must also possess the patience, persistence, and tenacity to perform accurately a never-ending set of tedious tasks. Many university libraries permit catalog-maintenance personnel to work on filing and removing cards for no more than several hours at a time to minimize mistakes due to fatigue.

The automated systems being used at our case-study sites did nothing to reduce the cost of maintenance activities. In fact, there was some evidence to suggest that the cost of catalog maintenance had actually increased as a result of the automated systems. Part of this effect was certainly transitory. Access to machine-readable catalog records created by other libraries encouraged our sites to undertake special projects to clear up cataloging arrearages that had accumulated before the data bases were available. The catalog cards generated by these projects just added to the normal volume of cards that had to be filed. Chicago, as we mentioned in chapter 2, had delayed cataloging numerous volumes until it could do so with MARC records. When the tapes were available, cards began to pour out of the system, leading to backlogs of unfiled cards that seemed insurmountable.

However, not all the reasons for the additional maintenance workload appeared to be transitory. Libraries that can produce catalog-card sets by pushing a button seem more inclined to update or correct already filed cards when more accurate records become available. This process, of course, adds not only to the task of card filing but also to the task of card removal.

University librarians undoubtedly recognize that the current use of automated systems to support cataloging is an interim stage in a transition to a full on-line catalog system. At present, automated systems are used to store and retrieve bibliographic information and produce the familiar three-by-five-inch catalog cards for manual filing. When university libraries close their catalogs, bibliographic information for all materials received subsequently will be stored in computer memory and accessed on-line. The task of catalog maintenance then will be dramatically revised and greatly simplified. But for most university libraries, on-line catalogs will not soon be available.

It seems certain that few university libraries will attempt to place their entire collections on-line. The cost of retrospectively converting all prior catalog records to machine-readable form is now prohibitive and will continue to be so for a while. Libraries will find it necessary to maintain the older manual card catalog. However, one can anticipate that the card catalog will, over the years, require fewer and fewer corrections and modifications. University libraries ultimately will enjoy the comparative ease of catalog maintenance for the ever-expanding volume of new on-line records. It seems quite certain that catalog maintenance is an activity that will undergo many fundamental transformations in the coming years.

Periodically, the cataloging rules change. The latest version, known as Anglo-American Cataloging Rules, Version II (AACR–II) went into effect 1 January 1981. It has been estimated that the entries of somewhere between 15 and 18 percent of the cards in the catalogs of academic libraries would have to be changed to comply with the new cataloging rules, and at least initially, up to 13 percent of the entries on newly filed cards would conflict with entries in the catalog.[3] Therefore, it makes sense to consider closing the old catalog and either beginning another or depending entirely on an on-line catalog.

Many university libraries originally planned to close their manual catalogs and put their new catalogs on-line with the implementation of AACR–II. However, few libraries had the capital to purchase the necessary software and hardware and operate the resulting system. Most have elected to begin new catalogs or to cope with filing new cards in existing card catalogs.

When a library puts its catalog on-line, it will not only need to have terminals for the technical and public-services staff, but it also will find it necessary to install a substantial number of terminals in public areas so that users can have access to the catalog as well. As catalogs go on-line, university libraries will be confronted with the formidable task of teaching users how to access bibliographic records via computer terminals. A comprehensive educational program and prompting devices will be required to assist various types of user, including undergraduates, graduate students, faculty, and research staff. University librarians will also be confronted with a challenging opportunity to include as part of this training remedial bibliographic instruction. Many librarians decry the underutilization of their resources, and it is widely speculated that one major cause for this neglect is widespread bibliographic ignorance. Teaching members of the university community to use the on-line catalog provides a marvelous opportunity to more generally raise the level of library literacy.

Serials

Differences in book and serials processing are primarily due to the continuing life of a serial. Unlike a book, a serial is never complete. Theoretically, there can be no last issue until a serial formally ceases publication. This fact means that a serials-acquisitions unit must be organized to monitor the receipt of titles with indefinite numbers of parts. It must also be geared to handle titles with varying schedules of publication because some serials publish frequently and over regular intervals, whereas some publish only sporadically.

A serials-cataloging unit must be prepared to maintain records that never close. Holdings must be updated when new volumes are bound. Catalog records must frequently be modified to incorporate changes in titles, publishers, editors, and even subject foci, because, unlike an edition of a book, a serial has no attribute that can be relied on to remain the same throughout the title's publication. Catalog records for books are not permanent; for example, newly established subjects may add points of entry to those in use or old entries may be judged obsolete. However, serials records are open to far more opportunities for change as a consequence of the continuing publication of the titles they represent.

Managing the incoming flow of serials is a major undertaking. Northwestern, the smallest of our sites, subscribes to 21,000 serials of which 15,000 are periodicals. If we assume an average frequency of four issues a year, periodicals alone account for 60,000 individual publications arriving annually—some 160 pieces daily.

Serials departments that have not automated the process of documenting receipt of pieces maintain card files, known as *serials records,* to aid in this task. The typical entry in a serials record notes all the issues of a title the library has received, including those that have been gathered in bound volumes. It may also note former or variant names of the serial, dates by which its parts usually arrive, the location of unbound issues and the call number of bound volumes, subscription details, the status of claims, and binding specifications. Some idea of the size of a serials record in a university library can be inferred from the number of serials university libraries handle. As can be seen in table 2-1, the libraries that participated in our study receive between 21,000 and 46,000 titles. A serials record would document a substantial portion of these currently received titles as well as titles no longer being received, either because subscriptions have been canceled or the titles have ceased publication.

A serials record and a public catalog are separately maintained files. In fact, the former is seldom available to the public but is kept within the serials-acquisitions unit. In figure 3-4, we indicate a link between the serials-acquisition function and reference. The serials record is primarily responsible for this relationship. It includes up-to-date information on currently received issues, data not available in publicly accessible files. Serials staff may be asked to retrieve these data. In fact, some serials departments, such as the one at the University of Washington library, maintain a public-service station for this purpose.

Another part of the information flow between serials processing and reference involves data about serials-in-process; that is, titles on order and in cataloging. On-line systems like NOTIS and the LDMS have the potential to decentralize access to these data, allowing item selectors, reference staff, branch librarians, and users to retrieve for themselves information on serials-in-process. Batch-processing systems also have this potential. Their data bases may be regularly output and disseminated in printed catalogs or on microfiche. In libraries with on-line access to in-process information or with regular distribution of in-process information through off-line vehicles, the need is lessening for technical-processing departments to participate directly in information retrieval for reference or item-selection purposes. In libraries like Northwestern that have also mechanized the receipt of current serials parts, it is disappearing entirely.

The relationship between acquisitions and circulation noted in figure 3-4 refers to acquisitions' role in directing pieces of a serial to their appropriate location in the library. Unlike books, serials are not as a rule ushered from processing to circulation through cataloging. Those responsible for noting the receipt of parts of a serial are also responsible for sending the parts to circulation areas. In fact serials-cataloging staff seldom see more

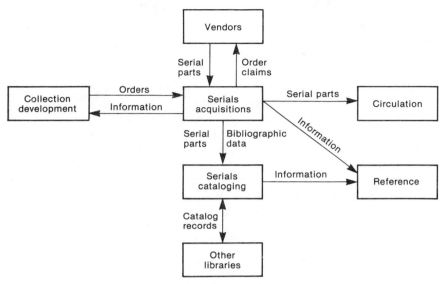

Figure 3-4. Serials

than the first piece of a new subscription, which is used to aid the title's cataloging.

Computer-based support for serials processing has a long history, beginning with systems to support acquisitions. In fact in the early 1960s, automation of serials acquisitions often was selected as a library's first automation project.[4] Aid for ordering new titles was seldom the focus of these early efforts, because new-title ordering accounts for only a fraction of the workload of serials acquisitions. The libraries in our study, for example, order on the average fewer than two thousand new titles a year. Rather, libraries concentrated on the considerably more time-consuming activities of recording the receipt of serial parts, identifying and claiming missing pieces, and identifying terminating subscriptions for renewal consideration. All these activities involve repetition of essentially the same clerical-level tasks, sometimes hundreds of times a day.

Consider monitoring the receipt of serials in a manually operated serials unit. For each of the hundreds of pieces received a day, a clerk must retrieve the card representing the title of the piece from a serials record of perhaps 20,000 or more cards, compare the bibliographic information on the card with that on the piece in hand, resolve discrepancies between the data or bring the discrepancies to the attention of his or her supervisor, and update the holdings data on the card to show that the library has received the piece.

With the thousands of pieces annually coming from numerous vendors, mistakes are inevitable. Vendors will mail issues to the wrong location or neglect to send them at all. They may send the wrong titles. Pieces will be lost or damaged in the mail. Insuring that the library receives all the pieces it is due requires systematic monitoring of the serials record. In fact, though, few university libraries can afford the personnel resources this activity demands. Instead, they rely on occasional sweeps of the serials record. They also rely on library personnel or users who report issues that they have unsuccessfully tried to find and check-in clerks who, while recording the receipt of a piece, discover that the library has not recorded a previously published issue. Not all lapses in service may be caught by these mechanisms, of course, at least not immediately. For example, one of our library participants undertook a systematic evaluation of the performance of a vendor after reviewing the list of titles the vendor was handling and noticing some peculiarities within it. The evaluation uncovered $15,000 worth of pieces the library had paid for but had never received.

The acquisitions activity for which computer-based tools can result in significant staff reductions is *claiming*. The process of check-in is made more efficient by automation, but even in automated environments staff are required to sort through the mail, compare incoming pieces with library records representing them, and initiate actions leading to record update. Claiming, however, can rely more heavily on the computer, which can systematically monitor the status of subscriptions, alert staff to lapses in service, and even generate appropriate claim notices and mailing labels. Ironically, libraries that have successfully automated the claiming process have seldom experienced significant staff reductions. As was suggested above, few libraries fully staff their claiming activity. Thus automated claiming systems have few people to replace. The major effect of claiming systems thus far has not been on staffing levels but on the library's capacity to monitor the incoming flow of serials. Automation has introduced a level of surveillance not possible before computer-based support.

The unpredictable behavior of serials has made automating their acquisition troublesome. In fact, many systems have been abandoned because of their inability to accommodate the idiosyncratic behavior of so many of the titles they are required to process.[5] Special or combined issues may arrive, frequencies may change, a one-time error or change in numbering may be made by a publisher. As has been mentioned before, reliable identifiers do not exist; titles, publishers, editors, subjects—all may and frequently do change.

The unpredictable behavior of serials has also plagued the development of systems to support serials cataloging. It was not until the mid-1970s that consensus on standards for communicating serials data was achieved, delayed primarily by lack of agreement over how uniquely to identify serials titles.[6] Even before consensus was reached, a major project called CONSER

(Conversion of Serials) was initiated by a small group of libraries, intent on building a comprehensive data base of serials records. The group thought that consensus on standards would emerge during, and indeed be encouraged by, the process of creating a national serials data base.

OCLC was selected as the repository for the data base, which was born in 1975. The file began with the Minnesota Union List of Serials and all machine-readable records that had thus far been created by LC. Ten institutions were selected to contribute further to the file. They were to enter the cataloging of their active serials, upgrading existing data or, if no data were found, entering original records. CONSER participants now number nineteen. In 1982, the CONSER data base included approximately 500,000 records. The Library of Congress and the National Library of Canada are responsible for quality control. Records authenticated by these institutions are distributed through the MARC distribution service.

The emergence of an acceptable standard for machine-readable serials records and the rapid growth of files of serials records based on this standard has encouraged the development of serials-order and serials-cataloging support systems tailored after and, in many cases, added onto those developed for books. Because of the similarity in the design of book- and serials-processing systems, changes in the organization of serials processing associated with automated systems parallel those that have occurred in book-processing units. However, they are not as noticeable because of the smaller volume of new orders and new cataloging associated with serials. For example, copy-cataloging units have not emerged as independent entities in serials departments. There is not enough copy cataloging going on to justify forming an independent unit.

Libraries maintain systems that inform users of the serials titles they receive and the particular pieces they own. However, few maintain systems that inform users of the contents of the serials they house, depending instead on indexing services to provide this information. Northwestern's transportation library is a rare exception. It regularly catalogs articles in serials and files the records in its public catalog. This single source of the library's holdings is a far more efficient and effective way for the library's users to explore what the library houses.

This kind of single-point access to a library's holdings may soon be more widespread. The Library of Congress is developing a machine-readable format for communicating data about articles in serials. Its issue and acceptance will certainly encourage libraries to catalog articles and, of course, share their records through the now numerous systems that disseminate machine-readable data. There already exists, of course, tremendous stores of machine-readable data representing articles. They are being exploited by the bibliographic-search services. Whether libraries will also be able to exploit these data remains to be seen.

Circulation

Circulation can be viewed as an end point in the technical processing of material. It is the final stop for books and serials flowing out of technical services. Circulation can also be viewed as an end point in the public-services workflow. Its stamp of approval is required before users can borrow the materials they have been directed to through public-service tools and personnel. A circulation department's direct contact with and participation in both technical and public services is responsible for the variation in its organizational location across libraries. As was noted in chapter 1, circulation is sometimes part of public services, sometimes part of technical services, and sometimes independent of both.

Actually the relationship between a circulation department and the library's users involves considerable more than the granting of permission to borrow material. Users approach the circulation desk for aid in locating material they have not been able to find on the shelves. Circulation departments regularly search the library for missing material. They also recall material on loan when it is needed by another user and hold material for the user when it is returned. Encouraging users to return borrowed items when loan periods expire is still another circulation activity. This task is accomplished primarily through a fine system, the management of which requires monitoring the circulation file for overdues, mailing out overdue notices, and maintaining an accounting system. Figure 3–5 summarizes the relationship between the circulation function and library users.

Circulation has in the past been a popular area for libraries to automate and continues to be so. Among library functions, it generally has been the easiest for systems analysts to understand because of its similarity to inventory control, a process that has been the focus of numerous automation efforts in commercial settings. Because of this similarity, it has also benefited more than other library activities from successful systems developed for commercial use. Circulation is isolated from other library activities, which has also contributed to its popularity as a site for automation. It can be automated without interfering with or altering the operations of other library units. Finally, circulation is a high-volume activity, laden with repetitive clerical tasks. Libraries circulating hundreds of thousands of titles a year can justify the cost of its mechanization with expectations of decreases in staff requirements and improvements in service.

The first mechanical device installed to aid the circulation process was a *card sorter,* implemented in 1936 at the University of Texas.[7] Over the next twenty-five years, libraries devised many ingenious ways to exploit card-sorting and collating equipment to aid in processing their circulation files. Card manipulators, though, did not aid the process of creating file entries—the records that link data about an item, its borrower, and the loan agree-

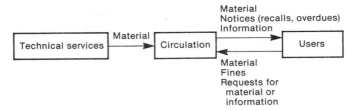

Figure 3-5. Circulation

ment. In fact, in many cases they complicated the task of record creation by requiring—for each circulation transaction—conversion of data into a machine-readable form.

By the 1960s, mechanized systems that automatically assembled circulation records, using data from sources identifying books and students, were widely available. Of course, the sources of identification had to be in machine-readable form, but they could be coded once and attached to books and student-identification cards for use in all subsequent transactions. As the decade came to a close, computers finally were introduced in circulation departments, replacing the card-sorting equipment that had been used to manipulate files. At that point, the typical computer-based circulation system relied on devices that automatically produced punched-card records of loans and returns.[8] At the end of the day, the deck of cards that had accumulated was taken to the computer center, where their data were merged into a master circulation file. A printout of the updated file was returned to the circulation department the next morning.

In the 1970s, on-line circulation systems started replacing batch-processing systems. The devices that assembled circulation records fed these data directly to a computer. The frequency with which on-line systems are found today is largely due to the many available turnkey circulation systems. The first turnkey system came to market in 1973. In 1979, Alice Bahr counted six commercial concerns selling stand-alone, minicomputer-based, on-line systems. She also noted several other vendors, including libraries, readying themselves for entry into this market.[9]

Most circulation files document material not in its proper shelf location. In chapter 1, we referred to such files as exception files. Of course most exception-file entries are items borrowed by students, faculty, and other library users. However, entries might also include items sent to the bindery, declared missing or lost, or temporarily moved to another area; for example, a collection of books placed on reserve. Manual circulation files are invariably exception files. Machine-readable circulation files include both exception and inventory files, the latter being files that contain records representing all circulating titles in the collection.

Implementing a computer-based circulation system is a tremendous undertaking, even when turnkey systems are purchased. If the system automatically creates circulation records, machine-readable identification must be attached to all items. If the system is based on an inventory file, a data base of records representing circulating titles must be created. New acquisitions can be bar-coded or supplied with punched cards as part of technical processing. Machine-readable records of new acquisitions for inventory files can also be generated as part of technical processing. But, how does a library affix identification to or include in inventory files all those volumes already in the collection?

Many libraries begin operating their circulation systems long before all items have been supplied with machine-readable identification. Chicago, for example, bar-coded only a fraction of the millions of volumes encompassed by its circulation system before the system was installed in 1978. When unlabeled material reached the circulation desk, desk attendants labeled the items as part of the loan transaction. Matching labels were placed on the book cards of the borrowed material, and the book cards were passed on to other circulation staff who updated an on-line file, the records of which linked bar codes to the call numbers of the volumes to which they were attached. At the time of our study, some 40 percent of borrowed material at Chicago was being labeled at the circulation desk. Already labeled volumes numbered about one million, or approximately 25 percent of the collection.

Although the bibliographic data entered in circulation inventory files can be less comprehensive than that needed for catalog files, the problems confronted when building inventory files are essentially the same as those encountered in constructing an on-line catalog. Most often the library's shelf list is relied on as the source of data about library holdings. The process of converting the shelf-list data to machine-readable form is now tremendously aided by the availability of large pools of machine-readable records; for example, the data base of OCLC. With access to such a pool, much manual inputting is avoided. Needed data can often be retrieved from the pool and copied into the library's inventory file.

As was suggested in our discussion of acquisitions, computer failures may completely halt critical book-processing activities in libraries with computer-based acquisitions and cataloging systems. Acquisitions departments relying on on-line in-process files cannot enter or update records or initiate the production of purchase orders or claims if the system stops functioning. They cannot search to insure that requested material is not already on order. Copy catalogers cannot search for machine-readable records created by other libraries. They cannot prepare final catalog records or order catalog-card sets.

In circulation departments with on-line circulation systems, failures may halt some activities, but they seldom stop the processing of loans. Manual systems of material check-out invariably back up on-line circulation systems. Libraries are most reluctant to tell users intent on borrowing material to wait until the circulation system is operating again.

However, circulation staff using on-line systems for loan transactions are far less tolerant of degradations in response time than are staff using on-line technical-service systems. In addition to their own exasperation when response time deteriorates, desk attendants must cope with the frustration and impatience of users waiting to conduct loan transactions. Chicago discovered, for example, that when 10 percent of the response times were greater than five seconds, staff generally found using the LDMS burdensome, particularly circulation staff.

Despite their concern for the continuity of service at the circulation desk libraries still experience public-relations problems when computer-based circulation systems fail. In comparison, manual backup systems are cumbersome. Furthermore, many users are often asked to employ manual procedures only after having already wasted time while circulation attendants unsuccessfully attempt to work with the on-line system. It is not uncommon for users to appear impatient and even angry when they are told they must conduct their loan transactions through manual procedures.

Automated circulation systems can support essentially all the clerical tasks circulation entails. They can automate the process of record creation, update, and purge. They can make more efficient the retrieval of particular records. They automatically can alert staff to overdues; block rights to borrow material; calculate fines; compute loan periods; alert staff to holds on returned material; and produce the numerous notices, slips, and receipts that circulation activities generate.

In addition, activated circulation systems can support activities usually considered a part of reference or collection development. Support of the reference function comes about with systems based on on-line or off-line inventory files. Such circulation systems have the potential to provide information on what the library has relative to a user's needs as well as its availability for loan. Some libraries have elected to provide subject access to circulation files to exploit more fully the reference capacity of their systems; they have in essence supplied their circulation systems with machine-readable catalogs. Salmon describes the Ohio State University circulation system, an excellent example of a system serving circulation and reference activities.[10] A more recent description is provided by Susan L. Miller.[11]

The use of circulation systems to aid collection development has been largely unrealized. What circulates should be of central concern to a library. It is an indicator of present needs and those of at least the immediate future. It is a measure of the success of past collection-development decisions. Because a major goal of a library is to respond to needs, it would seem that gathering and analyzing circulation data would be institutionalized in a library. However, libraries generally capture few data and make little use of what is collected. This fact may be due to the difficulty of collecting the kinds of data that would be beneficial to collection development. However, even in libraries with machine-readable circulation files, the development of software that would allow the regular analysis of collection use lags far behind software development in other areas.

Librarians are not short of ideas on how circulation data might be useful to collection development; their literature abounds with suggestions. John Martyn and F. Wilfred Lancaster provide an overview.[12] Perhaps as automated circulation systems mature more will be done to exploit their potential to shape collection-development policies. If so, one might expect to find still more variation in the organizational location of circulation departments in libraries. In addition to public and technical services, circulation might also turn up under the jurisdiction of collection-development officers. Indeed it can now be considered a legitimate part of collection management.

Reference

As mentioned in chapter 1, the purpose of reference services is to help users locate and use effectively materials from the library's holdings that are relevant to their research and instructional needs. As university libraries engage increasingly in shared collection development and interlibrary-loan activities, reference librarians more frequently help users retrieve material by other libraries as well. Reference departments are housed in public services and are composed of both professional and nonprofessional librarians.

These staff rotate the assignment of managing the reference desk, which is prominently located in one of the main public areas. At least one professional librarian is usually available at the reference desk and, during periods of peak activity, there may be more professional librarians on duty. These librarians may also have one or more assistants working with them to handle the more routine requests for service.

Unlike most other professionals in an academic library, reference librarians are subject to shift work, because the desk must be staffed during the evening and weekend hours. Consequently, it is rare to have all members of the reference department in the library at the same time. Reference librarians may spend fifteen to twenty hours per week on desk duty. The remainder of their time is devoted to other kinds of activities, such as compiling bibliographies, giving instruction, and preparing for or conducting on-line searches. Often reference librarians serve as part-time item selectors.

Reference librarians commonly distinguish between informational and reference questions. The former require no bibliographic source for their answer: Where is the pencil sharpener? When does the library close? I go to another school; can I use your library? Both librarians and support staff readily dispatch these kinds of requests for information.

Questions requiring consultation of a reference tool are more complex than informational questions and, therefore, more challenging intellectually. For example, a user might want to know if the library owns or is acquiring a particular item and when it will be available. He or she might wish to know if an item can be borrowed from another library. A user might want bibliographic information about a title for citation purposes or might desire a bibliography of all books and articles on a particular subject or by a particular author. As one might imagine, reference questions vary considerably in complexity. Some can be answered in minutes, while others might require hours.

Figure 3–6 is a schematic representation of reference services in a university library. As summarized in the upper portion of the figure, the major users of reference services are faculty, research staff, graduate students, and undergraduates. The last box in the top row represents the general public. Most private-university libraries actively discourage public use of the library through substantial charges for loan privileges, and some completely prohibit entrance to anyone without a university affiliation. Libraries in publicly supported institutions, particularly land-grant institutions, honor a long-standing tradition of providing services to the citizens, industries, and

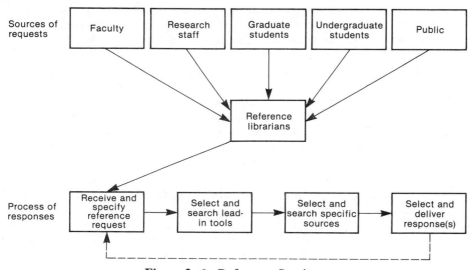

Figure 3-6. Reference Services

trade associations of their states. Many even manage extensively used state-wide networks of reference and interlibrary services and are appropriated substantial sums by their legislatures to support these programs.

Reference staff in public- and private-university libraries provide services to individuals affiliated with other universities; that is, the so-called community of scholars. There are many examples of formal agreements between universities giving mutual access to collections and services, such as those between Duke University and the University of North Carolina and between Stanford University and the University of California, Berkeley. A most extensive agreement is that among the RLG members.

In the bottom row of figure 3–6, we denote the major step in answering reference questions. The reference librarian must first understand precisely what the user desires. Through questioning, the librarian analyzes the request and identifies the kinds of information required. In many instances the reference librarian cannot answer the user's question without first consulting general sources of bibliographic information that in turn guide the librarian to more narrowly focused sources pertinent to the user's request. The second step in the reference process then is the selection and search of appropriate *lead-in tools*. There are three basic types of lead-in tools: card catalogs; literature guides, such as Sheehy's *Guide to Reference Books;*[13] and bibliographies, such as Brewer's *Dictionaries, Encyclopedias, and other Word-Related Books.*[14]

The third step in the reference process entails pursuing sources relevant to the user's query. The reference librarian might review, for example, monographs, serials, conference proceedings, indexes, subject bibliographies, abstracts, biographical directories, encyclopedias, dictionaries, atlases, gazetteers, guidebooks, annual reports, or yearbooks. The final step in the reference process is delivering a response to the user. Frequently, the response generates additional questions, and the process begins again. In some instances the user/librarian interaction may recycle many times.

In the rest of this section, we discuss three major areas in which automation has affected the delivery of reference services in university libraries. First, we discuss how reference librarians use on-line catalogs and in-process files. Next, we describe the use of on-line search services. Finally, we discuss the effect of automation on interlibrary-loan activities, particularly among the members of bibliographic cooperatives.

In libraries without on-line order and catalog data, reference librarians seeking information about local holdings consult the public catalog. For the status of or bibliographic data about items on order, they ask staff in technical services. For information about the holdings of other libraries, they consult union catalogs when they are available. Alternately, they write, telephone, or in some cases, telex their inquiries directly to other libraries. Data about the acquisitions of other libraries are seldom even pursued.

With on-line cataloging and acquisitions files, reference librarians can have immediate access to the in-process file of their library, as well as holdings that have been cataloged since the implementation of the system. Furthermore, reference staff in libraries participating in bibliographic cooperatives can also have immediate access to information on at least the recent holdings of member libraries, as well as their pending acquisitions. In sum, then, automated systems are giving reference librarians instant and single-source access to data previously available in numerous locations and often inconvenient or time-consuming to gather. These systems have decreased significantly the time needed to answer many kinds of reference questions and have encouraged librarians to answer more fully questions that were previously slighted because the data involved were burdensome to collect.

Reference librarians in university libraries increasingly are becoming involved in the use of on-line search services. There are now over one-hundred-and-fifty different files available among the various data-base vendors. However, there is substantial overlap in the files. There are basically two types of files included in the group. The first, and by far most common, are files of citations to publications. Most of the citations represent articles published in journals, but the files also include citations to monographs and unpublished technical reports, conference papers, and other fugitive documents. The second type of file contains data comparable to that available in handbooks; for example, *The Registry of Toxic Effects of Chemical Substances* or the *Grants Index,* which reports the granting activities of private foundations.

Many of the machine-readable files are created as a by-product of the computer-aided systems that produce printed versions of the data. Manual searching of the printed records depends on carefully constructed thesauri for access points, but the on-line search systems often permit more liberal access to the bibliographic files via words that appear in titles or abstracts. By using combinations of search terms more narrowly defined searches also can be completed. The efficiency and effectiveness of a search is highly dependent on familiarity with both the contents of a file and its search protocol, which may vary from file to file. Consequently, reference librarians tend to specialize in searching particular files.

The typical pattern for a search is as follows. The user schedules an appointment with the reference librarian who specializes in searching files appropriate to the user's substantive interests. During this appointment, the user discusses in detail the kinds of citations or information he or she is after. The librarian makes notes, usually consisting of preliminary search terms for accessing the files. Subsequently, the librarian refines the search strategy in consultation with system manuals and, perhaps, colleagues, and then sits down at a terminal and conducts the search. Some reference librarrians prefer to have the user present during the search, permitting the user to change either the terms or the overall strategy to sharpen the focus of the inquiry. The system indicates the number of records in a data file that has been retrieved as a result of a search term or combination of terms. In an interactive fashion, the search may be refined further until a manageable number of citations is indicated by the system.

During a search, the librarian may request printouts of several of the retrieved citations and abstracts to gain some knowledge of the effectiveness of the search strategy to that point. When a search is complete, the librarian may ask for an immediate printout of the retrieved citations. If the number of citations is substantial, however, this method is a costly way to display the search results. The librarian may also request an off-line printout, which is subsequently mailed by the data-base vendor to the library for delivery to the user.

Libraries are charged fees by the commercial services. They typically pass these costs on to the user. Costs for searches vary considerably, but reference librarians interviewed in the course of our field work indicated a fee of forty to fifty dollars was not unusual. Fees charged to the user usually recover only the amount that the vendor bills the library. In some instances, a small surcharge is added to help offset the cost of equipment rental and maintenance; but, rarely does a library try to recoup from users the total cost of a search, which would include the reference librarian's time.

Charging users for on-line searches makes a great many university librarians uncomfortable. On the one hand, there is a long standing and almost universally accepted principle in librarianship that information services should be made available to users free of charge. On the other hand, the costs of obtaining, using, and maintaining the on-line search services constitute a significant drain on the already severely pressed budgets of university libraries. Most university librarians have reluctantly acceded to these pressures by passing the direct costs of the searches on to the users.

Earlier, we presented our observations concerning the effect of on-line searches on the perceived professional status of librarians.[15] The interaction between librarians and users during traditionally administered reference encounters is fundamentally different from their interaction concerning an on-line search. In the latter case, librarians meet with users on an appointment basis rather than first come, first served. In addition, fees are charged. Consequently the user feels more justified in demanding a minimum level of satisfaction, and the librarian feels a heightened sense of responsibility for delivering a quality product. Because the end result of on-line searches is a printed record of citations, the librarian is acutely aware that his or her performance will be documented. Hence, many librarians spend a great deal of time preparing search strategies.

During our interviews, some reference librarians suggested still another

reason why their colleagues diligently prepare for searches—fear of en-
countering unmanageable situations during a search. Librarians gravitate to
reference work often because of their dislike for the more technical aspects
of librarianship as well as their desire to work with people. In fact for some
it is more than dislike; it is lack of confidence in their ability to master the
more technical aspects. For these individuals, conducting an on-line search,
often under the eye of the person paying for the search, is an uncomfortable
situation. To minimize their anxiety and the possibility of embarrassment,
they devote considerable attention to presearch activities.

There is currently a great deal of ambivalence on the part of many
university reference librarians concerning the future growth and development of on-line bibliographic-search services. As we just indicated, librarians spend more time preparing for and completing on-line bibliographic
searches than they typically devote to traditional reference encounters. Reference librarians fear that users who cannot afford on-line searches are
being unjustly treated by the library because, in comparison, little time is
devoted to their information needs. This discrepancy is one of the reasons
why many reference librarians are reluctant to publicize search services.

Some librarians anticipate a not-too-distant future when users will perform their own on-line searches. There is a difference of opinion among
librarians as to whether this development would be desirable. On the one
hand, some feel that it is unnecessary and impractical to duplicate the
expertise required to conduct searches among the many users of university
libraries. It is more efficient to centralize this proficiency. In fact, some
argue further that on-line search services might be delivered more economi-
cally by a number of regional centers. In contrast, other reference librarians, particularly those in the sciences, point out that most of their users are
already familiar with both the files they would explore and also computer
systems. It may well be that on-line searching will become a decentralized
activity in scientific and technical fields and continue to be executed centrally by the library staff in the humanities and some parts of the social
sciences.

At the University of Chicago and Northwestern University, reference
librarians used different terminals to access local files and the remote titles
of data-base vendors. At Stanford University, however, reference librarians
used the same terminals to search the RLIN files and the vendor files. Perhaps as a result reference librarians at Stanford made less of a distinction
between local and remote files, and they more readily transferred back and
forth.

Interlibrary loan is the third major area in which automation is affecting reference services. The records of bibliographic cooperatives indicate
member libraries that hold copies of the items. Thus libraries have a most
convenient way to locate possible sites for borrowing materials; they simply

check the on-line data base. Recognizing the usefulness of this feature in its system, OCLC installed a system that forwards interlibrary-loan requests to libraries. Members are supposed to respond to requests within a five-day working period. The sharing of resources through both interlibrary loans and on-site access is a major RLG program. Members use an electronic mail system to send loan requests to other members, and all have agreed to give priority to requests from RLG members.

In recent years, a number of large university libraries have instituted a procedure to recover the cost of interlibrary loans. This procedure is another radical departure from the tradition of free access to library materials, and it has also caused a deep division among librarians. Many librarians and administrators feel they can no longer divert scarce local resources to provide national and international lending services. Their libraries, therefore, charge for interlibrary loans. In addition, many libraries rigidly adhere to restrictive policies concerning what they will lend. Restrictive policies are strongly opposed by librarians who manage smaller collections and who depend on interlibrary loans to enrich local resources.

Some libraries simply do not have the manpower to cope with the numerous requests they receive for interlibrary loans. This shortage has spurred the birth of a new industry—private interlibrary-loan services. These entrepreneurial organizations are given access to a library's collection to respond to requests for material that can be copied. Frequently, these organizations consist of one or two persons to whom requests for materials are routed by the library staff. These individuals have free access to the stacks, and frequently they enjoy favorable copying rates. Because their operations are not affiliated officially with the library, at least part of the opposition to paying fees for retrieving and copying materials is deflected from the library to these small, quasi-independent organizations.

The evaluation of reference work is a controversial issue among university librarians. Many feel that the reference services they deliver are so diverse and tailored to individual users that developing systems to classify and measure meaningfully the value of their activities is virtually impossible. However, administrators in university libraries feel the pressure of diminishing financial resources and the growing concern for organizational accountability. Consequently they demand assessment of performance. Reference librarians for years now routinely have kept simple counts of the number of users served, distinguishing between their directional and bibliographic-information requests. Although these numbers routinely are recorded and published in annual reports, no one places much faith in these data as indicators of the level or quality of reference service.

The introduction of on-line systems to reference services provides an opportunity to assess systematically and more effectively the performance of reference librarians. The systems can be designed to include automatic audit records of reference activities. The amount of detailed information that might be accumulated and analyzed by these systems is immense. For example, it would be possible to record the number of times that inquiries were made by a particular reference librarian and the nature of each inquiry. It would also be possible to develop measures of the complexity of interactions. The cost of implementing automatic accounting or auditing trails of reference services would be substantial; but once in place, operational costs would be minimal. If such a capacity were developed centrally, perhaps by one of the cooperatives, its development costs could be dispersed among all the members.

Finally, with respect to automation in reference services, we will mention a new activity that may expand significantly the kinds of reference services university libraries routinely provide. Increasingly, libraries are becoming involved in the collection, storage, retrieval, and use of large-scale numerical data bases generated by government agencies, including the Social Security Administration, U.S. Bureau of the Census, and Bureau of Labor Statistics, as well as various private research agencies such as the Interuniversity Consortium for Political Research and the National Bureau of Economic Research. The computer programs commonly used to analyze the files are packages of general-purpose data-processing and statistical-analysis routines. The use of these files is one of the clear trends in social- and behavioral-science disciplines, and libraries seem to be positioning themselves to provide still another important service to their user communities.

Systems Activities

Numerous tasks are associated with selecting, implementing, and operating a computer-based system. Many are distinguished from other library activites in that they demand levels of computer expertise that, at least in the past, were not connected with training in librarianship. In this section we describe how libraries have responded to the need for computer expertise, focusing on the structure and operation of systems units.

It is misleading to associate systems activities with a particular library unit in the same way that one associates circulation tasks with a circulation department. First, libraries vary in the way they distribute responsibility for systems tasks between in-house staff and external individuals or organizations. Some, for example, retain little in-house expertise. They hire consultants to advise them on automation strategies, they look to the campus computer center for system designers and programmers, and they purchase commercially distributed and vendor-supported systems.

Second, libraries vary in how they identify those individuals within their organizations most associated with systems activities. Some libraries retain within a systems department what are called *systems analysts* or *systems librarians* or individuals with some other systems-prefixed title. Other libraries employ staff with systems titles, but these professionals reside within circulation, acquisitions, or cataloging departments. Still others employ no systems staff as such, but they rely on librarians in units affected by automation to accomplish systems-related tasks.

Even in libraries with formally designated systems departments, both systems personnel and librarians in departments affected by applications perform systems tasks. For example, a systems office may be responsible for selecting a circulation system, negotiating with its vendor, and coordinating its installation, while the circulation department is responsible for building the machine-readable reference files the system requires for its operation, attaching machine-readable identification to circulating volumes, teaching staff how to use the system, and preparing user manuals.

To illustrate further the difficulty in associating systems activities with a particular unit of the library, we will describe the organization of the systems function at each of the libraries that participated in our study, elaborating on the sketches provided in chapter 2. All of the libraries we visited retained full-time systems staff, and in all but Stanford they resided in systems departments. However, at each site the responsibility for systems tasks extended beyond systems personnel.

Figure 3–7 lists the major entities involved in systems activities at the University of Chicago library. They reside in two organizations, the library and the campus computer center. The library department formally identified with the systems function is the systems office. Actually, at the time of our study, the role of the systems office in LDMS activities was diminishing. During implementation, its staff had been immersed totally in LDMS-related activities. The office had been responsible for analyzing library functions for which automated support was planned, defining system requirements, directing system design, and overseeing system development and installation. During our study, the systems office was assuming some role in managing the operation of the LDMS, but systems staff were also taking on other projects with no particular relation to the LDMS. For example, one staff member, with partial funding from the Lilly Foundation, was exploring ways in which a group of theology libraries could produce a union catalog.

The operations coordinators noted in figure 3–7 were library staff who acted as links between those using the LDMS and computer-center staff responsible for its operation. Library staff reported to coordinators the problems they had with the system, which were categorized by the coordinators and conveyed to appropriate individuals in the center. The coordinators also disseminated to library staff information from the center. For example, they were assigned the responsibility of contacting the center dur-

Figure 3-7. Systems Participants—University of Chicago

ing a computer failure to obtain a forecast of the length of the outage. Subsequently, they would phone other library staff, who would in turn call others, and eventually all library staff using the system would be informed of the prediction. The library maintained several coordinators to insure that at least one was available during all hours of the system's operation.

The review committees listed in figure 3-7 were composed of systems-office staff and senior managers from technical and public services. They were responsible for giving priorities to the objectives of computer-center groups working with the LDMS, establishing levels of service the LDMS would provide, and initiating new work.

The committees started meeting when the development effort subsided and the library began to focus on the operation of the LDMS. In effect, the committees diluted the control the systems office had had over the computer center's design-and-programming group. As was mentioned in chapter 2, although the design-and-programming group was organizationally part of the computation center, it reported administratively to the systems office and in fact was located in the library. Before the formation of review committees, the systems office was, essentially, solely responsible for assigning and giving priorities to the tasks of the design-and-programming group.

Actually, the review committees were not composed entirely of library staff. The head of the design-and-programming group also sat on the committees. This person was, in fact, a central figure in the operation of the LDMS. He collected, organized, and presented most of the data the review committees used in their decision making. Indeed, he was largely responsible for devising the methods that led the committees to their decisions. As a committee member, he also had a voice in the decision making. Finally, in his capacity as head of the design-and-programming group, he assigned work activities to his unit and thus was responsible for interpreting guidelines established by the library.

During the implementation of the LDMS, the design-and-programming group had been charged with the design, implementation, operation, and maintenance of the application programs. Activities associated with operation and maintenance, though, were of lower priority, and numerous short-cuts and compromises were made to meet development deadlines and to respond to immediate operational needs. For example, some programming was left virtually undocumented. Problems or modifications involving these undocumented parts of the system required major work efforts because of the difficulty in understanding their function and operation.

At the time of our study, however, the emphasis of the group was changing—operation and maintenance tasks were taking precedence over development tasks. In fact, the group was reorganizing to function more effectively as an operation-and-maintenance unit. Just before our visit, it had changed its name to the Library Computer Systems Group, thus reflecting its new focus. Substructures were emerging in a previously undifferentiated group, distinguishing staff concerned with user support, maintenance, and operation from those responsible for new developments, with considerably more personnel resources allocated to the former activities.

In addition to insuring that the maintenance and operation of the LDMS would receive undivided attention, the departmentalization of the library-systems group put distance between those responsible for developing the system and its operation, a sometimes necessary separation. At Columbia University, for example, those responsible for building and enhancing the library's system were also responsible for its operation. Apparently, they had difficulty refraining from modifying portions of the operating system in response to suggestions from library staff or their own desire for improvements. The modifications often caused chaos in the library. Even changes perceived as trivial by programmers sometimes led to major system failures. The library finally resorted to dividing the systems department into two independent components, one of which was responsible for research and development, and the other for maintenance and operation of the on-going system.[16]

The other groups within the computer center of major importance to the operation of the LDMS were the data-base group and the communications-services group. The former was responsible for maintaining and enhancing the data-base management and the data-communications software upon which the LDMS relied, some of which was vendor supplied. The latter group was responsible for maintaining the library's terminals and the minicomputer housed in the library responsible for linking the terminals to the campus computer.

During the implementation of the LDMS, no central unit was formally responsible for coordinating the various entities charged with the operation of the LDMS—the design-and-programming group, the operations coordinators, those responsible for terminal maintenance, and those maintaining the data-management and communications systems. During our fieldwork, the design-and-programming group appeared to be assuming this responsibility. This change was adding further to the influence of the head of design and programming in the day-to-day operation of the LDMS.

The performance of library-systems tasks was considerably more centralized in the library at Northwestern than it was at the University of Chicago. The Northwestern library depended on the university administration's computer, and thus on its computer operators. It also depended on vendors and university technicians to maintain its terminals. However, library personnel performed essentially all other system activities.

Within the library, two units were identified formally with system activities—the systems department and the data center. The systems department was responsible for maintaining and operating NOTIS, as well as for designing, developing, and installing new system components. The head of the systems department was the principal liaison between the library and the administrative data-processing center. The department's systems analyst was the principal liaison between the systems department and library staff using NOTIS.

The systems analyst consulted directly with users on matters concerning system improvements, enhancements, and new system components. However, matters concerning the day-to-day operation of NOTIS were most often brought to the attention of the systems analyst by the head of the data center, the coordinator of automated procedures. The coordinator was in charge of user services—training others to use the system, preparing manuals, troubleshooting user problems, passing on to users information on system status, advising the systems analysts of the effects of proposed system changes and enhancements, alerting users to system changes, and helping supervisors integrate NOTIS into their procedures.

The head of the data center was most concerned with facilitating the use of NOTIS within technical services. In the late 1970s, when NOTIS was made available to public services, a need emerged for some kind of user support for reference, special-collection, and branch librarians. In fact, public-service librarians were agitating for their counterpart to the coordinator of automation procedures, and it appeared that a new position might be created. Public-service librarians were particularly concerned about the lack of training geared to their use of NOTIS, of manuals written from the point of view of public-service librarians, and of communication about system changes that affected their use of NOTIS.

Public-service librarians were also demanding and being granted more influence in the direction of NOTIS. The head of the reference department, for example, chaired a committee considering the future of the catalog, a committee created in 1978 to advise the library on the development of a publicly available on-line catalog. Systems and technical-services staff also sat on the committee, as did other public-service librarians. The group was assigned a number of tasks, including proposing terminal-screen formats, specifying the data to which users should have access, devising and evaluating various strategies to introduce the on-line catalog, proposing and evaluating alternate futures for the library's card catalogs, advising on the optimal location of the public terminals, and identifying other tasks and problems associated with what was anticipated as a forthcoming and radical change.

Northwestern's card-catalog committee had some similarity to Chicago's review committees. Both the card-catalog and review committees were formed to allow those using the system some voice in its direction. Both emerged late in the history of system implementation, and for some of the same reasons. Prior to their formation, the library administration and systems personnel at each site were preoccupied with development, as opposed to operational issues. Also, there was some delay before those using the system, especially those in public services, appreciated and became dismayed by the extent to which they had to adapt to changes over which they had esstentially no control. Finally, it took some time before librarians, again especially public-service librarians, gained the kind of technical knowledge that was needed for influencing systems-related decisions.

However, Chicago's review committees were far more powerful than Northwestern's card-catalog committee, playing a role in the day-to-day operation of existing system components as well as future developments. During the implementation of the LDMS, the cost of operating as well as developing the system was subsidized by external grants. When external funding ended, the library assumed the full burden of the system's cost. Monies to continue its operation had to be taken from monies allocated to other areas of the library. All at once decisions had to be made concerning the benefit of various levels of LDMS service relative to their cost. The review committees were born in the ensuing turmoil. Their formation and assigned role reflect both the participatory management ethos of the library and also the extent to which the system was used—essentially all areas of the library had to evaluate their use of the system and consider what they would give up to continue access.

As will be recalled, the development of Stanford's BALLOTS was initiated by the library but eventually became the responsibility of the campus computer center. However, throughout the system's evolution, library staff were involved in its implementation. The library director and the then associate director of technical services established priorities for the system's development. Senior and middle managers specified system requirements and helped in design. Staff in acquisitions and cataloging were called upon to put aside their normally assigned responsibilities to evaluate emerging system components and train other staff in their use. Although no one was associated formally with the systems function until 1978, many librarians participated in systems-related tasks.

In 1978, an individual who essentially knew more about the operation of BALLOTS than anyone else in the library was named systems librarian. Her expertise was an outgrowth of her involvement in evaluating prototype software packages and teaching others to use the system. However, the frequency of her selection by supervisors to participate in evaluation tasks and training activities, and the level of expertise she acquired, were due to her own intrinsic interest in automation and her desire to learn about the system. In fact, at each of our sites, as automation progressed, a few librarians who had previously known little about computers plunged into the automation effort and acquired, primarily through their own initative, skills in system use that exceeded those acquired by their colleagues. These individuals emerged as key actors in the operation of the system. They were sought after by colleagues when problems were encountered and depended upon by administrators for disseminating their knowledge to other system users. If the libraries chose to establish formal organizational entities related to system operation, the positions were filled by members of this group. In fact, it can be said that members from this group came to define these positions.

The systems librarian at Stanford was located in administrative services. Her role was similar to that of the coordinator of automated procedures at the Northwestern library. She helped supervisors develop new procedures that incorporated the use of RLIN; identified terminal problems and coordinated their repair; coordinated the installation or upgrade of equipment; trained staff to use the system; troubleshot user problems; and worked on special projects, such as the serials-conversion effort that was described in the Stanford profile.

She also was the principal liaison between the library and RLIN. Formally, she was supposed to work through RLIN's library-coordination department, which acted as the liaison between RLIN and the then eight RLG libraries. However, she seldom directed her communications to the library's assigned coordinator, choosing instead to consult directly with those in RLIN who could most apropriately address her problems. She bypassed the coordination department in part because it was perceived then as ineffective. Also, she knew the RLIN organization well, having worked with many of its staff during the BALLOTS implementation; and she had little need for guidance through its rather complex structure. At that time RLIN had some sixty staff members.

The systems librarian primarily focused on the needs of technical services. In fact, until shortly before our visit, she resided in the technical-services division. At the time of our study, the Stanford library was planning to hire a second systems librarian, who would facilitate the use of RLIN within public services. The situation was similar to that observed at Northwestern. In both cases, the computer-based systems became available to public-services librarians long after they had been installed in technical-services locations. The user support structures that evolved were geared to facilitate technical services' use of the system. Public-services librarians resented this bias and eventually demanded attention to their particular needs.

The Stanford library has always depended on external organizations for the operation and maintenance of its system. At present, RLG assumes this responsibility. The library, however, plays a direct role in managing the computer facility it uses, although its control is shared with other RLG members. RLG library directors, for example, form the board of governors, the policy-setting arm of the RLG. Specifications for new or modified system components must be reviewed and approved by RLG members before they are implemented. In fact, staff from member libraries often join RLG systems personnel in formulating these specifications. Also, through a standing advisory committee, RLG members can initiate work on system improvements, enhancements, and new developments. Actually, a number of standing committees meet, covering the range of library concerns. RLG libraries are represented by staff selected because of their expertise in the areas of concern to the committees. Four major committees now serve RLG—collection management, shared resources, material preservation, and technical services.

Like Stanford, the University of Washington library relies to a large extent on external organizations for the operation and maintenance of the systems it uses. As will be recalled, the library maintained memberships in both OCLC and WLN at the time of our study. Unlike Stanford, though, the library played essentially no role in the direction of the bibliographic cooperatives of which it was a part. Like most members of bibliographic cooperatives, the Washington library was just a consumer of the cooperatives' services.

The library maintained a systems office, but its staff did not participate in WLN or OCLC affairs beyond coordinating the installation of terminals. Supervisors in units using the systems were responsible for integrating the use of WLN and OCLC into procedures, training others to use the systems, and contacting and negotiating with network organizations about operational problems. The library director was responsible for determining the extent to which the library would use the services of bibliographic cooperatives, naming the units that would have access to the systems, and prescribing the services they could use. The director also played a role in integrating the use of the systems into library tasks. As will be recalled the heads of the technical-services departments reported both to the director and to a coordinator of bibliographic control. The library director was formally responsible for setting policy. However, his participation in frequent meetings of technical-service managers led to his involvement in implementing policy as well.

The descriptions given above of the organization of the systems function at each of our sites illustrate the variation one may observe both across institutions and within an institution over time. Northwestern was the most self-sufficient of our sites, depending least on external organizations to perform systems-related tasks. In this sense, it had the most control over its system. Chicago, Stanford, and Washington all depended more heavily on external parties.

Chicago, Northwestern, and Washington maintained systems departments, but only Chicago's was staffed entirely with librarians. The others included non-librarian computer experts—systems analysts, programmers, software designers. However, the need for libraries to look beyond the pool of librarians for inhouse computer expertise seems to be diminishing and may disappear entirely. The decreasing need for outside expertise is due in part to the growing sophistication of librarians with computers. It is also due to the lessening requirements for inhouse expertise. The level of expertise required by libraries is being lowered by the growing market of systems and by the now-widespread availability of information characterizing, evaluating, and comparing competing alternatives. Libraries can now shop for computer support. They no longer have to resort to inhouse development projects. Also, external organizations offering libraries the computer expertise they require abound. University libraries can turn to campus computer centers, private consultations having extensive experience with computer-based library tools, commercial vendors catering to library needs, regional network organizations, and the bibliographic cooperatives.

Structure and Authority

In complex organizations authority, or the right to decide how others will behave in their work, is distributed throughout the structure created by the division of labor. Authority is delegated from the chief executive officer to all supervisors, giving them total control over the job performance of their staff. From one perspective, ultimate authority is derived from the consent and cooperation of the supervised rather than from managers.[17] The distribution of authority in organizations is further complicated when specialized knowledge is introduced into the organization to improve goal accomplishment. This outcome is particularly true when that knowledge is not shared by all organization members. As Francis Bacon noted long ago, knowledge is power. In his studies of industries, Alvin Gouldner noted that specialized knowledge or expertise frequently bestows additional authority upon individuals.[18]

In our case studies we encountered instances of this phenomenon. For example, in one library the supervisor of circulation records reported that one of the biggest changes she experienced with automation of the circulation department was the greater distance she perceived between herself and day-to-day operations. There were many technical details associated with operating the automated system, details that could only be understood by those who worked with the system on a day-to-day basis. In her words, she had become more of a generalist while her staff were the specialists. She felt that she had to maintain a general knowledge of the system as a whole to coordinate the activities of the various units she supervised. However, she did not have the time to learn about the system in more detail. Thus, she could not closely supervise the specifics of the system operation.

In this particular example, automation resulted in more individuals sharing authority. However, automation does not always result in decentralizing authority. For example, automated technical-service systems employ a central bibliographic-data file. To work with this file most efficiently the various units in acquisitions and cataloging have to devise procedures that output data consistent with division-wide standards. This kind of change can be viewed as a centralization of authority.

A third change in the distribution of authority that may accompany automation is a lateral shift. This shift is observed, for example, in libraries that rely on outside agencies for services and expertise. In these libraries, procedures and policies previously established locally may be influenced, and in some cases determined, by the outside agencies. This shifting of authority to another organization is causing the traditional boundaries of libraries to become less distinct and therefore less clearly recognized.

One could argue that the boundaries of university libraries were never very clearly demarcated. Many of their policies and operating procedures have been determined by host institutions. In this sense, university libraries have never been totally autonomous units. However, automation, coupled with increased resource sharing, is further dissolving the boundaries that have separated libraries from other organizations.

Changes in the distribution of authority are leading indicators of forthcoming structural shifts and functional reorganizations within libraries. From one perspective, authority is the day-to-day manifestation of structure in complex organizations. Changes in structure always lag behind changes in authority. The many changes in authority that we detected in our case-study libraries lead us to speculate that organizational shifts will become more and more apparent in university libraries.

Notes

1. For a more complete discussion, see Hugh F. Cline and Loraine T. Sinnott, *Building Library Collections,* p. 130.

2. Ibid., p. 99.

3. Arlene T. Dowell, "A Five-Year Projection of the Impact of the Rules for Form of Heading in the Anglo-American Cataloging Rules, 2nd Edition, upon Selected Academic Library Catalogs.

4. See Barbara G. Toohill, *Guide to Library Automation,* p. 85.

5. See Stephen R. Salmon, *Library Automation Systems,* p. 148.

6. Ibid., p. 169.

7. Ibid., p. 188.

8. Ibid., pp. 188–211.

9. See Alice H. Bahr, *Automated Circulation Systems, 1979–80,* p. 10.

10. Salmon, *Library Automation Systems,* pp. 206–208.

11. Susan L. Miller, "The Evolution of an On-line Catalog," pp. 193–204.

12. John Martyn and F. Wilfred Lancaster, *Investigative Methods in Library and Information Science,* pp. 97–106.

13. Eugene P. Sheehy, *Guide to Reference Books.*

14. Annie M. Brewer, ed., *Dictionaries, Encyclopedias, and Other Word-Related Books, 1966–1974.*

15. Cline and Sinnott, *Building Library Collections,* pp. 138–140.

16. Paul J. Fasana, "The Columbia Experience," p. 14.

17. Chester I. Barnard, *The Functions of the Executive,* p. 163.

18. Alvin Gouldner, *Patterns of Industrial Bureaucracy,* pp. 9–24.

4   Information

We turn now to the information dimension of organization analysis. As we remarked in the introductory chapter, considering this dimension entails viewing an organization as a collection of decision makers connected via data-transmission channels. In studies of complex organizations, the information dimension is commonly referred to as *communication patterns,* and usually these patterns are viewed from three perspectives. The first is *vertical,* a perception of information transmission between hierarchical levels of the organization. The second viewpoint is *lateral,* a view of communication between organization members across different units or departments. The third perspective encompasses information transmitted *beyond the boundaries* of the organization.

A separate but related distinction often noted in the literature is that between formal and informal patterns of communication. This theoretical distinction can be stated readily: the former pertains to messages whose content is related to organizational functioning; the latter refers usually to messages of little or no relevance to organizational goal accomplishment.[1] Informal communications are commonly lateral. Although informal patterns are important, especially as determinants of the social climate of complex organizations, we shall focus here primarily, if not exclusively, on patterns of formal communication, both within the library and between the library and other organizations.

In chapter 3, we discussed how organizations group related tasks and assign individuals responsibility for performing some or all of the tasks in a group. Connected to this division of labor is a network of decision makers. The distribution of authority to implement decisions is represented in both the organization chart and job descriptions. Organizations evolve systems for monitoring the flow of data within their boundaries to insure that decision makers have timely access to information pertinent to their activities. Supervisors at every level need to be intensely concerned with the adequate flow of information along all data channels, both those within the organization and those between the organization and its environment.

To examine the information dimension, investigators must first identify the key decision makers in the organization and then map the data channels connecting them. Having plotted this network, the investigator might then tap a sample of the communication lines to observe the frequency of their use and the content of the transmissions. This intervention is probably the most difficult and sensitive aspect of case studies, for the investigator must attempt to balance the need to gather relevant information with consideration for the legitimate rights of persons and organizations to maintain individual and collective privacy. Tapping the communication lines can be done by observing or participating in organization activities. These methods, of course, are traditionally employed by social anthropologists. It requires a great deal of time and is in many instances extremely expensive. Consequently, only a small amount of participant observation was employed in the present study. The investigator can, as an alternative, ask organization members in personal interviews to serve as so-called informants concerning the content and frequency of their own communication activities. This option was more attractive and hence was employed extensively in our comparative case studies.

In the review that follows, we explore four topics related to the information dimension. First, we map the information networks of our case-study libraries, using data collected in our interviews. These networks will be depicted in diagrams and then compared across libraries. Second, we examine patterns of information transfer within each library to identify changes related to introducing automated systems, including communications within and between technical-service units, public-service units, and systems departments. Third, we review patterns of communication between libraries and other organizations, including bibliographic cooperatives, resource-sharing consortia, funding agencies, commercial vendors, and the like. Finally, we review evidence, collected in the four case studies, suggesting that new patterns of information transfer may be emerging in university libraries, patterns that result partially from increasing involvement in automation. We conclude this discussion with a review of the implications of these changing patterns of communication and comment on an organizational structure that eventually may become prevalent in university libraries.

Sociometric Analysis

As sociological cartographers, we wanted to map the information networks of our case-study libraries. To do this we employed the techniques of sociometry, first devised by J.L. Moreno in the 1940s[2] and subsequently expanded and adopted in many different kinds of organizations. Sociometry uses a method of data collection and analysis to portray relationships among members of a group. Children may be asked, for example, to name classmates with whom they play at recess. Totaling the number of times a child is chosen as a playmate produces a measure of popularity. Counting the number of choices a child makes produces a measure of *extroversion*. Through various matrix manipulations, more complex questions about the group structure can be explored, such as the extent of mutual choices and clique structures.[3]

The sociometric data are usually coded into square matrixes, with row and column headings representing interviewees. Table 4-1 portrays an example of a hypothetical sociometric-data matrix created for illustrative purposes. In the matrix appearing at the top of the table, each cell is uniquely identified with two numbers representing row and column positions, respectively; that is, 1-1 denotes the first row and first column and 4-5 the fourth row and fifth column. Hypothetical sociometric data are entered in the matrix in the bottom half of the table. For example, Jones names Smith, Thomas, and Miller, but not Jackson. A "one" is placed in cells 2-1, 3-1, and 4-1; and "zero" is placed in cell 5-1. The first column, then, reflects Jones's choices. Smith, on the other hand, chooses only Jones and Thomas. Therefore, a "one" is placed in cells 1-2, and 3-2; and "zero" is placed in 4-2 and 5-2. In this manner, the second column portrays Smith's choice; and the third, fourth, and fifth columns denote Thomas's, Miller's, and Jackson's choices, respectively. Note that X is placed in all diagonal cells of the matrix, for self-choice has no meaning in this type of analysis.

Using this small example we can illustrate some simple sociometric analyses. Column totals represent the number of individuals named. Row

Table 4-1
Example of a Sociometric-Data Matrix

	Jones	Smith	Thomas	Miller	Jackson	
Jones	1-1	1-2	1-3	1-4	1-5	
Smith	2-1	2-2	2-3	2-4	2-5	
Thomas	3-1	3-2	3-3	3-4	3-5	
Miller	4-1	4-2	4-3	4-4	4-5	
Jackson	5-1	5-2	5-3	5-4	5-5	
	Jones	Smith	Thomas	Miller	Jackson	Total
Jones	X	1	1	1	0	3
Smith	1	X	1	1	0	3
Thomas	1	1	X	1	1	4
Miller	1	0	1	X	0	2
Jackson	0	0	1	0	X	1
Total	3	2	4	3	1	—

totals present choices received. Thomas appears to be a central figure in the network, naming and being named by all of its participants. Jackson, on the other hand, appears to be of lesser sociometric importance. Of course, the interpretation of the data depends on the relationship under study. If group members had been asked, "Whom do you hang out with?", the data would reflect popularity. If group members had been asked, "Whom do you interact with in order to do your job?", the data would reflect indispensability to the information flow of the unit.

In a sociometric matrix of five individuals, there are twenty (five times four) possible choices. The proportion of choices made is a rough indicator of the group's interconnectedness. In our example, we see by adding the row or column totals that thirteen choices were made, rendering an interconnectedness measure of thirteen divided by twenty, or 65 percent.

We can also illustrate the concept of symmetry in sociometric-data analyses. A symmetrical choice is a reciprocated choice; that is, Jones chooses Smith (a "one" in cell 2-1) and Smith chooses Jones (a "one" in cell 1-2). An asymmetrical choice is a one-way or nonreciprocated choice; that is, Miller chooses Smith (a "one" in cell 2-4), but Smith does not choose Miller (a "zero" in cell 4-2).

At the University of Chicago, the subject of our first field visit, we asked interviewees to name other library-staff members from whom they would seek information under several different hypothetical situations, as in a breakdown of the computer system. It quickly became obvious that the hypothetical situations varied in pertinence across Chicago's library units. We therefore abandoned our sociometric questions and any effort at a sociometric analysis of the Chicago library staff.

In the remaining three institutions, we asked interviewees only to list the names of colleagues with whom they frequently interacted on job-related matters. Almost all interviewees enjoyed answering this question, and they often spent considerable time in elaborating on their responses. We made no suggestions of how many individuals should be named, for we were also interested in the interviewees' perceptions of the size of their information networks.

At each institution we completed approximately fifty interviews with library staff. In several instances it was, however, not possible to obtain a satisfactory response to the sociometric question. The first row in table 4–2 indicates the number of persons from whom sociometric data were forthcoming. With few exceptions, those from whom we received the data were members of the professional staff. The second row in table 4–2 indicates the size of the professional staff in each library, and the third row indicates the percentage of professional staff represented in our sociometric networks.

As can be seen, the University of Washington library received the least coverage. This result is due primarily to the large number of branches in the central system. We interviewed librarians from only ten of the nineteen

Table 4-2
Sociometric-Data Summary

	Northwestern	Stanford	Washington
Completed sociometric question	46	43	47
Professional staff	80	75	121
Proportion of professional staff who completed sociometric question	57.5%	57.3%	38.8%
Average number of choices	7.96	6.81	6.60

branch libraries. In particular, librarians from the law and medical libraries were not part of our interview schedule. They account for thirty of Washington's professional staff. As we mentioned in chapter 2, their counterparts at Northwestern and Stanford are not part of the central systems on these campuses. The Northwestern and Stanford personnel data in table 4-2 include only those units within the central system.

Across the sites, we strove to interview staff in parallel positions; that is, middle managers in technical and public services, branch librarians responsible for comparable areas of the collection. Thus the content of our sociometric networks as measured by positions included was more or less equivalent across the sites.

The fourth row of data in table 4-2 displays the average number of individuals within a network who were named by a network member. As can be seen, those interviewed at Northwestern tended to name more individuals than their counterparts at Stanford and Washington, a reflection of greater interaction prevailing within the Northwestern interpersonal network.

Social scientists have devised a variety of techniques for examining sociometric-data matrixes. As a first step toward their interpretation, matrixes are often simplified or reduced in size. We began our analysis by reducing the size of each matrix until it included only those designated by their peers as most critical in the information flow. This end was achieved by iteratively removing from each matrix all those named by their colleagues three or fewer times. Three choices was slightly less than half the average number of times an individual was selected, as table 4-2 demonstrates.

Each matrix was therefore reduced by using row totals; that is, choices received. The row and column of anyone whose row sum was less than four was removed. New row totals were then calculated on the reduced matrix. Again, those having fewer than four nominations were eliminated. This process was repeated until no further reductions occurred. After four repetitions, the Northwestern matrix reduced to twenty-eight persons. The

Washington matrix reduced to twenty-four persons after three repetitions. The Stanford matrix reduced to twenty-two persons after two repetitions.

We further simplified the matrixes by retaining only symmetrical entries; that is, a "one" in a cell was dropped if it was not matched across the matrix diagonal by another "one". At the end of these deletions, several individuals were not named by any of his or her colleagues in the structure of which they were a part. They were dropped from the matrixes, thus leaving the Northwestern matrix with twenty-seven individuals and those of Washington and Stanford with twenty-one.

Figures 4–1, 4–2, and 4–3 present the resulting matrix data, translated into three sociometric diagrams. The nodes in these figures represent individuals. The library director is designated by an encircled D. Dotted nodes represent individuals in public services; white circles represent technical-service staff; and lined circles represent individuals assigned to administrative, personnel, or systems units. Adjacent to each node is an abbreviation of the individual's position. The key to these designators is provided below each figure. An asterisk next to an abbreviation indicates the individual is the head of his unit. Thus TS* denotes the head of technical services. Connecting lines indicate that the individuals represented by the circles interact in the course of their job performance. We remind the reader that only symmetrical ties are represented.

Some features of the diagrams will now be highlighted. Within the Northwestern diagram are many more ties between public- and technical-services staff than appear in the diagrams representing the other institutions. The tightly interwoven substructure of bibliographers and acquisitions staff accounts for much of this interaction. A link can be found between almost every pair of individuals in the substructure. The higher level of communication between technical and public services at Northwestern may reflect the more mature stage of evolution of NOTIS toward a library-wide system, depended on by both technical- and public-service librarians.

Notice that at Northwestern the director is linked to seven other individuals. Three of these are in public services and one is within technical services. The content of this substructure contrasts with the substructure of which the director of the University of Washington library is a part. As figure 4–3 shows, the Washington director also interacts with seven individuals, but four are in technical services and only one is in public services. The director of the Washington library was, at the time of our study, immersed in the automation of technical services. His communication patterns reflect his level of involvement. Perhaps as automation progresses at Washington, the director's ties to middle managers in technical services will weaken. Northwestern's director, on the other hand, was more concerned with expanding the use of NOTIS within public services, and his relatively larger number of contacts with public-service librarians reflects this focus.

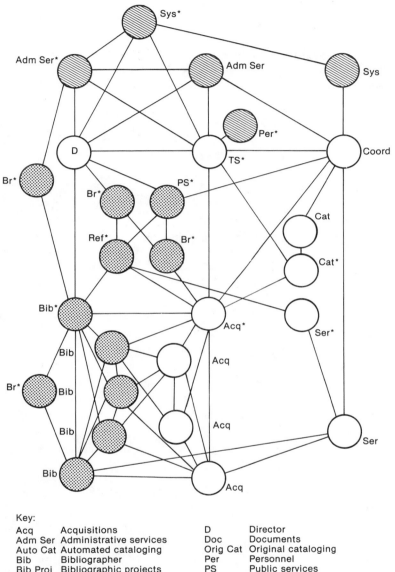

Key:

Acq	Acquisitions	D	Director
Adm Ser	Administrative services	Doc	Documents
Auto Cat	Automated cataloging	Orig Cat	Original cataloging
Bib	Bibliographer	Per	Personnel
Bib Proj	Bibliographic projects	PS	Public services
Br	Branch librarian	Ref	Reference
Bud	Budget officer	Sci Div	Science division
Cat	Cataloging	Ser	Serials
Cir	Circulation	Sys	Systems
Coord	Coordinator of automation	TS	Technical services

*Indicates head of unit.

Figure 4-1. Sociometric Diagram for the Northwestern Library

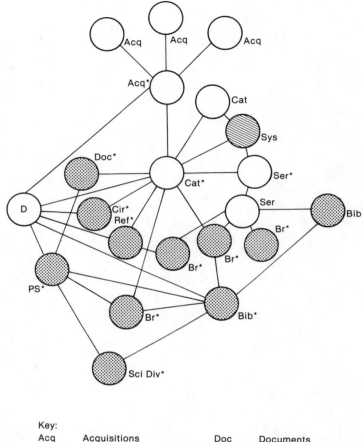

Figure 4–2. Sociometric Diagram for the Stanford Library

The Stanford director has a total of six contacts in his network. Four of these are in public services: the head of circulation, the head of reference, the chief bibliographer, and the head of public services. He has two contacts within technical services, the head of acquisitions and the head of cataloging, who at the time of our study was also functioning as the head of technical services. Like the Northwestern director, the bulk of the Stanford

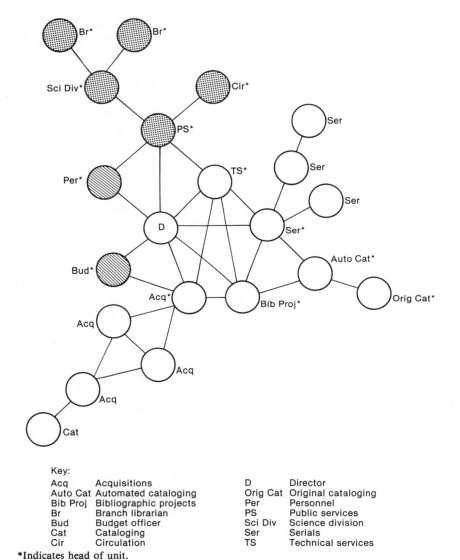

Key:

Acq	Acquisitions	D	Director
Auto Cat	Automated cataloging	Orig Cat	Original cataloging
Bib Proj	Bibliographic projects	Per	Personnel
Br	Branch librarian	PS	Public services
Bud	Budget officer	Sci Div	Science division
Cat	Cataloging	Ser	Serials
Cir	Circulation	TS	Technical services

*Indicates head of unit.

Figure 4–3. Sociometric Diagram for the University of Washington Library

director's contacts are in public services, and this pattern may represent a more mature automated system that is functioning more or less smoothly within technical-service units and is now beginning to branch out to public-service units.

If we compare the sociometric position of systems personnel in these three institutions, we note first that this function is most prominent at Northwestern. The two individuals within the network designated as *Sys* are members of the systems department, the head of the unit and the systems analyst. User services, it will be recalled, is the domain of the individual designated as *Coord,* the coordinator of automation for technical services. As the Northwestern diagram shows, the coordinator is linked directly to technical-services units using the system, as reflected by her ties to acquisitions, cataloging, and serials personnel. The systems department is linked to the users by the coordinators. The head of the systems department is linked to the director, the heads of administrative and technical services, and the systems analyst.

At the University of Washington, the systems personnel do not appear in the diagram at all. As mentioned previously, the two-person systems department is not participating in the computer activities that have been introduced recently by the new director. These individuals are working with off-line systems and have little to do with the planning for new on-line automated systems. The five persons most heavily engaged in planning for these systems are those occupying the central pentagon in the Washington diagram, including the director and the heads of technical-services operations, serials, acquisitions, and bibliographic projects.

At Stanford there is only one systems position in the library. The person holding this position is involved in user services and formally assigned to the administrative-services unit. In the sociometric network, this individual is linked to key staff in technical services, including the acting director of technical services and the heads of serials and automated cataloging. This pattern of interaction is entirely consistent with the use of RLIN at the time of our study. At that time it was primarily a tool for technical services—a tool that had only recently begun to be used by public services.

The Stanford diagram suggests that the head of cataloging plays a pivotal role in the library's communications structure. The number of links to this node is ten, the largest number of links emanating from any of the nodes in the three diagrams. Several factors contribute to the central role played by this person. The first is that she was, at the time of our study, also acting head of technical services. Also contributing to her centrality is the size of the cataloging department, which employs a total of fifty-five individuals serving in eleven subunits, many of which are linked strongly to public-service units. For example, both the documents and undergraduate cataloging sections frequently interact with their public-service counterparts. Finally, support of cataloging was a central concern of RLIN at the time of our study. The cataloging department's long involvement with BALLOTS implementation combined with its central role in RLIN's use undoubtedly contributed to the influence of the head of cataloging in the communications structure of the library.

The almost complete star structure in the middle of the University of Washington representation suggests the existence of a core of individuals through whom information flows to various parts of the library. Thus, for example, information to public services appears to go through the head of public services, and information to members of the acquisitions department appears to travel through the head of that department. The director of the library is a member of the central pentagon, all the other members of which are from technical services. Other interesting features of the Washington network are the relative sociometric distance between technical- and public-service units, and the relative isolation of the various units in technical services. Both features, we suspect, are characteristics of manually operated libraries, and the diagram indeed gives evidence for the appropriateness of our having chosen the University of Washington as a library whose automation activities have just gotten underway.

Internal Communication Patterns

In this section we discuss changing communication patterns within the library resulting from automation, patterns reported to us in the interviews. The data for our analyses came primarily to us through responses to questions about the respondents' job functions and activities. Most commonly, respondents reported that automation had produced more frequent contacts, closer interaction, and better understanding among the various units in technical services and circulation than had existed previously.

In manual libraries, circulation and technical-service departments, and frequently units within these departments, maintain their own paper files to monitor the flow of materials. In those university libraries that employ automated systems, such as Chicago, Northwestern, and Stanford, the need for independently maintained files diminishes as units can rely on centralized on-line data. However, the various units maintaining and using the on-line files must employ common standards and definitions, a requirement that lends to more communication across units concerning their internal procedures. In a manual setting, for example, if a section does not like the form of the output being generated by another, the receiving section can just build another file that transforms the incoming data into a tolerable form. In an automated setting, the sections must arrive at mutually acceptable standards because they are forced to work with common record formats and files.

In automated settings, data created by staff generally have more visibility than data created in manual settings. If entered into on-line files, the input is available immediately to all those with access to a terminal. We were not able to determine whether the larger audience for one's output has affected its quality or quantity. Some librarians expressed feelings of discomfort with the new level of self-exposure. Richard DeGennaro has observed a similar phenomenon on a more general level. He contends that original catalogers contributing to the data bases of bibliographic cooperatives have become self-conscious as a result of the widespread distribution of their records. This self-consciousness, he claims, has had a debilitating effect on productivity.[4]

Our interviews uncovered change in communications between technical- and public-service units. Libraries often maintain a small unit within technical services charged with facilitating the flow of materials among the various stations in the technical-processing workflow. The *distribution unit,* as it may be called, is also responsible for locating specific material in response to queries from those outside of technical services. At Chicago, Northwestern, and Stanford, however, the on-line files maintain up-to-date information on the location of in-process items. At these sites the distribution unit is no longer the best source for location data—and certainly not the most convenient when a terminal is available. Librarians have come to rely on the system rather than distribution personnel for such information.

Distribution staff, however, often provide more than location information when contacted. They also pursue more specific questions on anticipated status change. Many public-service librarians with access to automated systems are also bypassing distribution staff when seeking information on anticipated time in processing, contacting instead the station said by the system to have possession of the material. This change has generated problems, with staff in technical services, especially catalogers, expressing dismay over interruptions in their work to answer questions about when they might complete work on a particular item. It was not clear at the time of our study whether library managers would attempt to discourage those direct contacts with technical-services staff. It was clear that automated systems significantly had increased the visibility of technical-services operations to public-services librarians, allowing them to monitor directly the progress or, as some would contend, lack of progress of their item selections through technical processing.

Perhaps because of a paucity of interaction or because of communications that may not be understood by all parties involved, the staff of systems departments are frequently perceived as being guarded in their discussions with other library staff. This attitude is reported to be particularly evident when systems people are asked questions about future changes or enhancements. On the other hand, systems staff, who frequently feel overburdened, recognize that they may not always take the time necessary to explain or to give full answers to queries. Furthermore, most library managers and systems staff are acutely aware of the need to manage change as effectively and efficiently as possible. Thus they may be reluctant to discuss upcoming changes with a single interlocutor until appropriate announcements have been made and briefings held for all affected staff.

A particularly interesting pattern of communication between the systems department and the circulation department evolved at the University of Chicago when the automated circulation system was installed. During the many months of system design, much interaction occurred between circulation and systems personnel. All supervisors and many desk clerks had been involved in numerous design meetings, and a close working relationship developed between the two units. When the system became operational, the supervisors in circulation decided to permit systems-department staff to communicate directly with colleagues at all levels in the department, since channeling interactions through supervisors would be less efficient. This pattern certainly facilitated the introduction of the circulation system; but as a by-product, many among the support staff in circulation felt they now had multiple supervisors—one in circulation and several more in systems—a perception that aroused consternation. As the system became operational and immediate difficulties decreased, multiple supervision also appeared to diminish as a problem. Nevertheless, dual hierarchy still emerges as an issue whenever a systems tangle develops.

When we attempt to identify changes in communication that can be attributed to automation, sorting out the permanent from the temporary is particularly difficult. The automation itself will inevitably change. System components will be enhanced or modified, and some will become obsolete and be replaced. New functions will be encompassed by automation; new functions will be born. Because of the instability of automation one might expect permanent patterns of communication to be rare in automated environments. Indeed, stable communication patterns may well be lost once automation is introduced.

External Communication Patterns

In reporting changes in patterns of communication between libraries and other organizations, we find it convenient to divide the interactions into two categories. The first category is that of communication between the library and other organizations within the university. The second category covers communication between the library and organizations outside the university, such as the bibliographic cooperatives, other resource-sharing consortia, funding agencies, commercial vendors, and professional associations.

When the library shares the use of a centralized campus computing facility, a most dramatic change occurs in communications with the computing center. Before library functions were automated, virtually no communication between the library and computer center had taken place. With the advent of a locally supported computer system, of course, communication between the library and center begins. Their interaction is most intense during the installation phase of the system and then wanes as start-up problems are resolved.

Libraries that rely upon the local computing center for time-sharing services present a set of problems very different from those of typical university-computer-center users. For example, libraries operate on schedules varying from twelve to twenty-four hours per day, and typically they operate over weekends, holidays, and vacations. Most other computer-center users are accustomed to having computer services at least curtailed during other than normal business hours. Most university computing centers are oriented primarily toward having their machines used for rapid and large-scale manipulation of numerical data. Libraries, on the other hand, deal primarily with textual data. The traditional user of the university computing center tends to require relatively small portions of time for input-output operations and uses the greatest amount of time for internal processing. Libraries present the opposite pattern. Processing time tends to be minimal, and input-output operations are more common, more time-consuming, and usually more expensive. Finally, and perhaps most importantly, computing center and library staff originate from very different cultures and often have difficulty communicating effectively. Computing-center staff are likely to come from mathematical, operations-research, or systems backgrounds. Librarians for the most part have backgrounds in the nonquantitative disciplines. Seldom do these groups share common objectives, perspectives, or even vocabulary.

Whether the computer used by the library resides on or off campus, the pattern and content of communications between the library and faculty usually are affected profoundly by automation. Effective university librarians recognize that their primary constituency is the campus faculty. Whenever changes occur in library operations, prudent librarians are especially assiduous in their efforts to inform faculty about the rationale and anticipated benefits of the changes. To ignore this responsibility is to court disaster. A conflict can develop if faculty are not convinced that automation will improve library services that support the university's research and instructional programs. For example, unless faculty believe that automation will improve services, they are apt to resent investing large sums in hardware and software when the acquisitions budget is insufficient. Despite librarians' sincere efforts, professors, especially in the humanities, often persist in criticizing what they view as the squandering of scarce funds on futile computer systems. This inherent and continuing tension between advocates of collection development and advocates of automated systems is likely to continue and to require both understanding and patient diplomacy from university librarians.

In addition to the computing center and faculty, the university administration is another unit whose communications with the library are affected by automation. Because substantial funding is needed to support library automation, the university administration becomes involved more intimately with the library's fiscal situation. This fact is true whether the university provides the money or accepts the funding from outside agencies. A new accountability relationship to the administration evolves, and existing communication patterns are altered as a result.

Many automated systems perform book-fund posting and produce payment vouchers. However, check writing, one of the most routine applications of automated systems, has not been implemented in computer-supported library systems. Apparently, it has proved difficult to link the fund-disbursement system of the university administration and the automated library system. It is safe to assume that this link will someday be made and that communications between fund accounting and disbursing units will be automated eventually.

Finally, with respect to the university's internal communications, the use of automated systems to support library operations frequently gives rise to a new link between the library and the university maintenance and physical plant units. Installation of computers, terminals, printers, and the like frequently entails special construction, wiring, security, and temperature and humidity controls. Interactions tend to be most intense during periods of planning and installation, but maintenance also requires periodic communication between library and physical-plant staff.

Changes in communications between the library and external groups will now be considered. The bibliographic cooperatives, OCLC, RLIN, and WLN, are probably the most important of these organizations. Members of these cooperatives now experience an intense new form of communication, arising from the numerous daily requests for on-line bibliographic information. In addition, librarians in technical- and public-service units interact with individuals in the central office of the cooperative, regional organizations brokering cooperative services, and other member libraries. Perhaps the most routinized type of communication among member libraries is that associated with interlibrary loans. The on-line bibliographic files make it possible to identify which member libraries hold a particular book and both RLIN and OCLC further provide the capacity for on-line requests of materials.

The bibliographic cooperatives, and in particular OCLC and WLN, have increased the number of libraries participating in interlibrary loans. Before the cooperatives, the National Union Catalog and New Serials Titles were the only location tools generally available to the library community, and their coverage of libraries included for the most part major research libraries. Furthermore, many libraries did not purchase these tools because of their expense; they sent requests to major libraries in their area just on the chance that the rich collections contained the sought-after-material.

In the OCLC and WLN data bases, even the smallest members announce their holdings, making it feasible to identify nonresearch libraries as sites from which to borrow material. In fact, nonresearch libraries are frequently found to be more convenient sources of material. They more often have the requested material on the shelf and can deliver material more quickly, presumably because of their relatively lighter interlibrary-loan volume.

Another relationship that did not exist before the advent of computer-aided systems is the connection between libraries and commercial vendors providing turnkey systems or access to remotely located data bases. Of the four libraries included in this investigation, the only contractual arrangements between the libraries and commercial vendors involving computer-aided systems were those with on-line bibliographic-search services. None of our case-study libraries were using turnkey systems. We do, nevertheless, know from reports of staff members at other academic libraries that when such systems are first installed, the interaction between library staff and the commercial vendor is intense. Generally, this level of interaction is renewed when the system fails and a crew is needed to repair the system. Because a system failure usually brings some part of the library's operations to a halt, strong pressure is usually generated to effect the repair as rapidly as possible. During these times, communications are frequently strained.

The relationship between a commercial vendor of a system and the library is considerably more formal than the relationship that evolves between the library and a systems department responsible for a locally developed system. With a vendor a contract is drawn, which may outline the library's expectations of system performance as well as specify the system's cost and delivery dates. Systems personnel are not legally obligated to fulfill the commitments they may make to the library. Of course, there may well be negative repercussions if systems personnel fail to perform adequately, but it is unlikely that litigation would result. Also the lines of interaction between a commercial vendor and the library essentially match those summarized in the organization chart, with vendor/library communications for the most part handled by senior and middle managers. Systems and library personnel, as was suggested in the above discussion of Chicago's circulation system, for the most part disregard the chain of command, or formal authority structure, dealing directly with those most affected by or concerned with the communication.

Regarding interaction with the purveyors of on-line bibliographic-search services, we note with some surprise that except for initial contract negotiations and subsequent training of staff members to conduct on-line searches, interactions with personnel employed by the search services are minimal. The staff, of course, frequently interact with the system in conducting the searches, but bills, system news, publications, and the like are communicated through the mails or through system announcements.

Patterns of communication between university libraries and the Library of Congress have been profoundly affected by automation. Institutions like Chicago and Northwestern, which maintain their own technical-services systems, receive weekly tapes from LC containing the recently completed and released MARC records. Stanford and the University of Washington gain access to these MARC records through their respective bibliographic cooperatives. With MARC, LC has significantly influenced the design of computer-aided library systems. Also, LC has frequently convened cross-institutional policy groups and working committees to address automation-related issues. For example, under the auspices of LC, the Network Advisory Group, comprising national leaders in the library-automation field, is exploring the feasibility of linking the now independent bibliographic cooperatives to form a unifed national network.

Three other organizations will be described. Each plays a unique role in the library field, and each has made or has the potential to make a major contribution to library automation. The first is the Council on Library Resources. Established with initial support from the Ford Foundation, the council is a private foundation situated in Washington, D.C. Its general mandate is to improve the operation of libraries within the United States. Until recently, the council was concerned with all types of libraries, including university, college, research, public, industrial, and school. Now the council is focusing more on the specific problems of university and research libraries. The council has served as a most effective fund-raising agency for the Research Libraries Group. It has helped raise from private foundations millions of dollars to support the recent RLG expansion from three to twenty-six members. The council directs a five million dollar project, established in 1978, called the Bibliographic Service Development Program. The project's goal is to improve bibliographic services, with particular attention to controlling the cost of their delivery in individual libraries. The council is at present providing support and direction for automation activities that will affect university and research libraries significantly in the future.

A second organization of critical importance to the library community is the Center for Research Libraries. Established just after World War II, the center is a membership organization to which some one-hundred college, university, and industrial libraries belong. The purpose of the center is to improve resource sharing among member libraries. By accepting donations from member libraries or purchasing collections, the center has built a collection of over a million volumes of often rare and expensive materials. Individuals associated with member libraries can borrow these materials at very low cost. Materials may be retained indefinitely or until they are requested by another member library. By sharing these large and expensive collections, the center can reduce the aquisitions budget of all member libraries. Members pay an annual fee calculated on a sliding scale that reflects the library's size.

The Center for Research Libraries has recently embarked on a new type of resource-sharing activity involving serials. It intends to become a national serials-lending center, a concept explored and promoted for several years by the Council on Library Resources.[5] The center will build a collection of about 60,000 serials titles and will sell copies of articles at cost. A national periodicals center has been operational in Great Britain for several years, and users report great satisfaction with its services. If rapid document delivery can be achieved by the center, it is possible that it can help university libraries by reducing their current-serials commitments, especially to the less frequently used journals. From the university library's viewpoint, this reliance on the center would be highly desirable; the implications for publishers of serials are, however, devastating.

The third organization, the National Commission on Libraries and Information Science (NCLIS), was established in the 1960s by presidential order. The commission was charged with planning national policy for library and information services. Unfortunately, NCLIS has become bogged down in politics, professional as well as presidential. Its vision of the future of information science has been restricted by more immediate concerns. NCLIS thus has yet to become an important factor in the development of automated library systems.

Matrix Management

As has been suggested before, automation is a continually changing process. System components are modified, enhanced, replaced, and expanded. New ways to exploit them are discovered. New services based on their use emerge. This instability leads to another form of instability—instability in communication patterns. When a branch library is given a terminal, the branch librarian's immediate access to acquisitions and cataloging data will likely alter his or her relationship with technical-services personnel. If current holdings of serials are added to bibliographic records, public-service librarians may no longer need to consult with serials librarians to determine if a particular issue has been received. When a library joins a cooperative, links to external organizations proliferate.

Among the organizational changes introduced by automation continually changing patterns of communication may be the most profound. The comparatively stable patterns of communication that characterize manually operated libraries are lost. Coping with constant change in communications requires an organization to develop a more fluid structure, capable of accommodating the frequently changing relationships among divisions, departments, units within departments, and individuals within units.[6] Over ten years ago, Alvin Toffler described one organizational response to continuing change in communication patterns, He coined the terms *adhocracy* to describe the shift from a traditional bureaucracy to a more flexible format in which individuals are assigned permanently to administrative departments and temporarily to specific projects.[7] The temporary project assignments give rise to a second, coexisting organizational structure, frequently referred to as *project* or *matrix management.*

Matrix management introduces a two-dimensional management structure. Individuals are assigned to two locations in an organization. The first location corresponds to their assignment to a department or unit in the formal table of organization. The second corresponds to one or several project teams, committees, or task forces, the latter assignments varying in duration and intensity of involvement.

An example of one form of matrix management exists at the Rand Corporation, an independent nonprofit organization that conducts research on a variety of topics in the social and behavioral sciences. In addition to several administrative units, the formal organization at Rand consists of six departments: computer services, economics, engineering and applied sciences, information sciences, management sciences, and social sciences. Overlaid on this departmental structure are three research divisions corresponding to the projects undertaken by the corporation: project Air Force, national-security research, and domestic research. Each department has a chairperson, and each research division is supervised by a vice-president. Research divisions are further divided into project areas. For example, domestic research includes criminal justice, education and human resources, energy policy, health sciences, housing and urban policy, labor and population, and regulatory policies and institutions.[8]

A scientist at Rand is affiliated with one department and reports to the chair of that department for administrative and personnel matters. Furthermore, he or she may be working on one or more individual research projects and report to the heads of the units who oversee the projects for substantive research-related activities. Individuals rarely change their departmental assignment, but their assignment to projects and research divisions are in constant flux as specific projects are planned, executed, and phased out.

In university libraries, the proliferation of project committees, task forces, and the like suggests the emergence of matrix management. Although libraries depended on such groups before automation, their use has increased in recent years, at least partially as a result of automation. So many automation-related issues extend beyond the concern of a single organizational unit. University librarians now serve with increasing frequency on groups concerned with, for example, the future of the card catalog, the review of system specifications, the coordination of bibliographic-search services, the evaluation of system performance, and the preparation of user manuals. To our knowledge, no university library has formally instituted a matrix structure. However, increasing temporary or permanent assignment of personnel to groups whose membership is drawn from various departments may be another harbinger of major changes forthcoming in the traditional organization of libraries.

Notes

1. See Chester I. Barnard, *The Functions of the Executive,* pp. 114–123, 217–227.
2. See J.L. Moreno, "Experimental Sociometry and the Experimental Method in Science"; and J.L. Moreno, *Who Shall Survive?*
3. For examples of more recent and sophisticated sociometric analyses, see Samuel Leinhardt, ed., *Social Networks.*
4. See Richard DeGennaro, "Libraries and Networks in Transition," p. 1046.
5. Council on Library Resources, Inc. *A National Periodicals Center Technical Development Plan.*
6. For an excellent discussion on this point, see Paul S. Goodman, ed., *Change in Organizations.*
7. Alvin Toffler, *Future Shock,* pp. 112–135.
8. *Rand Corporation Annual Report* (Santa Monica, Calif.: 1981), p. 105.

5   Fiscal

The fiscal dimension of organizational analysis encompasses the activities related to the acquisition, allocation, and expenditure of monetary resources to accomplish organizational goals. It is concerned with both the short-range perspective; that is, current expenditures, and the long-range; that is, capital investment in improvements to the physical plant or a computer to support automated systems.

Budget making provides the foundation for other fiscal activities. Because a university library is a unit within a larger organization, its budget process is part of the host institution's budgeting, wherein a finite sum each year must support many different enterprises; for example, the library, instructional programs, research institutes, and athletic departments. The process of allocating university monies to each of these units is usually highly political, with the university administration presiding over the competition for funds. The budget-making process within the library is also one in which different units (for example, bibliographers, reference, and circulation) compete for resources, and the library administration attends to the husbanding of library resources. Units within the university frequently undertake entrepreneurial activities to increase their revenues. Thus an academic program may add a revenue-producing adult-education course; a computer center may sell services or software; or the library may collect lending fees from outside users.

The budgets of most state-supported universities are approved yearly by the legislature. Funds not spent by the end of the fiscal year often cannot be carried over as credit for the next year but must be returned to the state's general fund. Administrators in these institutions do not want to lose appropriated funds. Consequently, they compare budgets and expenditures throughout the fiscal year. Whenever they see substantial discrepancies accumulating, they adjust expense levels or revise budgets. Hence, a library may find its budget substantially altered as it enters the last quarter of a fiscal year.

All university libraries employ some method of accounting for expenditures, and these records are usually available for inspection. Nevertheless, investigators must be alert to outlays not reported in normal fund-accounting statements. For example, money for purchasing rare books and other expensive items commonly is donated to university libraries. The expenditure of these donations is rarely anticipated in budgets and frequently not documented in accounting statements. Such activities must be anticipated if the fiscal dimension is to be more accurately represented than is customary in library-budget and accounting statements.

In this chapter, we inspect patterns of funding for automated activities in university libraries and examine the varying effects these patterns have on the library's fiscal relationship to its host institution. It is important to recognize that university administrators view library computing activities in the broader context of university-wide computation in support of all instructional, research, and administrative functions. Thus, requests for computers to support automated activities in libraries are viewed by host-institution administrators in the context of campus-wide requirements for computing resources.

Also in this chapter we review the difficulties of estimating the costs and benefits of automated systems, scrutinizing the problem of assessing nonquantitative benefits. After briefly examining the effect of automation on the physical plant of the library, we discuss the various forms and functions of systems departments and comment on long-range fiscal planning for automation. We concentrate here on mechanisms used to design and effect enhancements to automated systems. In the final section we suggest that automation is rarely a single-step task of installing a computer system; rather, it is a continuous sequence of refinement and enhancement.

Funding

When a university library develops or obtains an automated system to support operations, its fiscal procedures are profoundly affected. This outcome is true regardless of whether the system is developed locally, obtained from an outside commercial source, or provided through membership in a bibliographic cooperative. In automating any aspect of their operations, university libraries typically incur a large initial expense associated with obtaining, installing, and starting-up a system—as well as continuing expenses for maintenance and enhancements.

A limited number of options are available to university libraries for obtaining start-up and continuing funds to support automation. We have defined seven options, five of which involve the use of university resources. These are:

1. a budget increase granted by the host institution,
2. a budget transfer in which the library decreases expenditures in one category to offset new or increased expenditures for automated systems,

3. a loan from the host institution to be paid back from the future cost savings,
4. the sale of library holdings, and
5. the collection of fees from users of the automated systems.

The other two options involve the acquisition of external funds; that is, grants and contracts.

From the perspective of the library director, a budget increase granted by the host institution is probably the preferred option. The institution merely increases the library's budget to compensate for additional costs, and the library is obligated to the host institution only for the delivery of an effective system. Institutional budget increases have been used to pay for the development of local systems, the acquisition of commercial systems, and the membership costs of participating in a bibliographic utility. Frequently, budget increases are granted when an addition is made to the physical plant of the library, either in the form of a new wing to an existing building or of a totally new facility. The approval of such physical-plant expansion usually includes allocations for furnishings, such as computer hardware.

Budget transfers are often employed by university libraries to offset automation costs. They rarely provide sufficient monies to cover all the expenses associated with the acquisition or development of a major library system, but they can be used to obtain a more limited support system.

As economic conditions in universities continue to worsen during the 1980s, it will be increasingly difficult to depend either on budget increases or on transfers to finance library automation. Competition for limited funds among all units within universities will surely intensify, and as a consequence funds for increases or transfers will diminish.

Some university libraries have used the method of borrowing on future budgets to raise the funds necessary for initiating automation. Generally, these loans are granted in expectation of future cost savings, usually in the form of personnel reduction. Repayments frequently are calculated in constant dollars, thus sparing the library some of the devastating effects of inflation. One may question whether many loans will ever be fully repaid. Automated systems do not necessarily produce substantial savings leading to budget reductions. A more common pattern is for services to expand while costs remain much the same. To be sure, this situation may be temporary, and cost savings through staff reductions or lower operating expenses may one day be realized. For the present, however, it must be acknowledged that many loan repayments to host institution are subject to indefinite delays.

A fourth source of internal funds is the sale of valuable items in the library's collection for the specific purpose of raising capital for automation. University libraries have, for example, sold rare books, paintings, coins, and stamps. Ten years ago, the sale of such collectables would have been most unusual. Librarians who exercise this option for raising funds explain that they dispose of valuable items in their possession that have only minimal value for scholarly research. Furthermore, they point out that secure storage of these items is an increasing drain on the library and a deflection of its resources away from the primary goal of providing access to materials that support the institution's research and instructional programs.

The fifth option for funding library automation is fee collection. As already mentioned, levying fees is a practice most university libraries employ reluctantly, for free services in libraries is a time-honored tradition. For the most part, user fees are now restricted to reference services provided with on-line commercial systems. The library usually charges only for the direct costs of the search, as billed by the supplier. Occasionally, libraries do add surcharges to recover administrative and personnel costs, but even these charges rarely generate substantial income. Nevertheless, fees for the commercial services continue almost uniformly to be passed on to the user.

An interesting comparison can be drawn between university libraries and computer centers with respect to user fees. A brief history of the relationships between university computing centers and their funding sources is illuminating. In the early 1960s, major U.S. research universities established central computing centers. Hardware manufacturers, most notably IBM, lent universities their new second-generation computers at no charge. Their intention, of course, was to introduce their products to students and faculty, who would in turn become future clients. But it quickly became obvious, even to a corporation the size of IBM, that the cost of providing a large second-generation mainframe to every major university in the country was prohibitive. The free-loan policy consequently was replaced by an educational-discount policy. The universities then turned to the federal government for support of computing.

During those years, federal grants to support both higher education and scientific research were growing exponentially. Research universities turned mainly to the Office of Computing Activities (OCA) at the National Science Foundation for money to support campus computing. As a consequence of this support, faculty and students had access to free and essentially unlimited computer time. The computer center was able to provide hardware, systems, operators, and some software support. Users supplied their own programming.

By 1965, OCA realized that it could no longer continue to pay for computer hardware for even the major research universities. Thus, universities seeking money for third-generation hardware in order to capitalize on increased miniaturization, reliability, processing speed, and on-line storage capacities had to be refused.

The disappearance of federal support meant that computing had to become self-supporting. Administrators therefore devised a system for supporting computer centers that combined revenues from several sources, including the basic university budget, user fees, and various other income-producing schemes. Free and unlimited computing disappeared permanently, and payment for computer services was firmly established.

Today, most centers operate with income generated from many sources. Students, faculty, administrators, research staff, and outside clients expect to pay for computing time, although universities, in fact, continue to subsidize limited amounts of computer time for instructional programs and for the unfunded research of students. A major source of support is grants or contracts that include computing costs in their budgets. Although it is obviously an important goal for universities to offer ready access to computers, users pay for services rendered.

On the other hand, the tradition of free library services is a venerable one and is firmly entrenched as an ideal. However, the skyrocketing costs of maintaining and expanding university libraries can no longer be borne primarily by host institutions. Automation provides new opportunities to introduce appropriate levels of user fees especially for services substantially improved by computer-aided systems. Many librarians expected that users would object to paying fees for the commercial search service. In fact, little faculty or student opposition has been reported. Many apparently believe that the service rendered is so far superior to manual searches that they are quite willing to pay the tolls. University administrators and library directors might seek the advice of fiscal managers and planners to develop other kinds of fee structures that can help offset the costs of future library operation and automation.

Funding for automated systems is also available through external grants and contracts. Most university libraries routinely seek outside grants from public and private agencies to support many activities, including automation. At one time, federal funding agencies provided support to university libraries seeking computer hardware and wishing to develop software systems. However, as we have already noted, these agencies now refrain from such help. They prefer instead to support activities that potentially have application in many university libraries rather than in a single institution.

Private foundations also support the automation activities of libraries. For example, W.K. Kellogg Foundation has assisted libraries in the Midwest to defray the costs of joining the OCLC network. In most instances, these funds, grants of about five-thousand dollars each, were given to smaller college libraries to obtain terminals and pay the initial costs of converting to the OCLC automated catalog-card system. More recently, several private foundations, through the Council on Library Resources, have given money to the Research Libraries Group to assist libraries in meeting the costs of joining the RLIN network. These funds are used as an incentive to join and as compensation for obtaining terminals, participating in various committees, and preparing machine-readable versions of bibliographic descriptions of the library's holdings.

The final funding option is contracts with outside agencies. For example, libraries and corporations may contract to develop jointly an automated system that they will subsequently sell or lease to other libraries. A variant of the contract source of funding is found in libraries that have made contracts with their state governments to provide interlibrary-loan or reference services to libraries throughout the state. For example, the University of Wisconsin, the University of Minnesota, and the University of Virginia, among others, currently receive funding for statewide lending and reference services. Support is typically in the form of a reimbursement for each transaction. However, some library directors have effectively used these reimbursements to support automated activities that further improve local as well as statewide delivery of library services.

The option or combination of options adopted by a library to obtain money for automation has direct implications for the library's obligations to deliver completed and efficiently functioning systems. The primary distinction is that between money obtained internally and that obtained from external sources. In the former case, the library is obligated only to itself and its host institution to provide the automated services as promised. As a result of a long history of previous interactions, the library staff is knowledgeable in and adept at dealing with obligations to their local administrators. Universities normally do not have extensive reporting requirements for internally funded library-automation projects.

It frequently happens that other units within the university, particularly faculty, may believe that local resources used to support library-automation activities should be used to support other activities, collection development, for example. If faculty consider that monies spent to support automation are funds diverted from already-shrinking book budgets, hostility toward the library may be rapidly generated—particularly if there is little visible evidence that the automated systems will have direct utility for the faculty. The potential for this kind of acute reaction from the faculty occurs when automated activities primarily support technical services, services with little visibility outside the library.

The potential for negative reaction from the administration or faculty is particularly great if budget increases or loans on future budgets are used as a means of financing automation. If a transfer is made with the library, there is less likelihood that a negative reaction will result, simply because the internal budget transfer is essentially invisible to individuals not on the library staff. However, staff in units within the library whose budgets have been decreased to provide funds for automation may become hostile or angry because their units were selected to pay the bill for automation.

In summary, using internal funding options for automation provides several advantages—flexibility and few reporting requirements—and one important disadvantage—the potential for generating hostility within the user community and the library staff. With external support, university libraries almost always experience additional and sometimes onerous reporting requirements, such as the interim and final reports demanded by funding agencies. The library will often experience pressures to meet all these reporting requirements from both the funding agency and the university administration, which usually acts as fiscal agent for the grant as well as intermediary for the funding agency. Some university libraries are therefore reluctant to enter into outside grant arrangements.

Another problem is that in the course of developing automated systems, libraries frequently discover that modifications to the original plan are necessary. The difficulty arises that many outside granting agencies have fairly elaborate and cumbersome procedures for making changes. Flexibility in developing projects is thus often severely curtailed. Of course, the degree of flexibility varies from one granting agency to another; but library directors have become more and more aware of how difficult it is to work with external agencies, whether their subsidies come in the form of a grant or a contract.

Costs and Benefits

Whenever substantial sums, whatever their source, are employed to initiate, maintain, or expand a program in an organization, it is an axiom of good management to determine that the costs involved do not exceed the long-range benefits to be derived from the investment. Suggested techniques for estimating costs and benefits are amply documented. In for-profit organizations, dollars can be used as a unit of measurement of both expenses and profits. However, in nonprofit organizations, particularly those engaged in delivering services, it is often exceedingly difficult to put a monetary value on benefits. How does one measure in dollars improvements in medical care, compensatory education, academic-degree programs, or library services?

During the 1960s, cost-benefit analyses were fashionable, particularly in government agencies. Tremendous enthusiasm was generated for approaches that were variously labeled cost-benefit analysis; systems analysis; and planning, programming and budgeting (PPB).[1] The widespread attempts to apply the concept of cost benefit to all sorts of programs in government agencies and nonprofit organizations gave rise to rather acrimonious debates.[2] Many proponents oversold the value of their approach to the assessment of new programs and frequently attempted to place numerical values on program outputs that were not readily amenable to quantification. The critics pointed out that social indicators and extrapolations of nonlinear curves contributed little to understanding the outcomes of most service programs.

These debates were useful, for a certain degree of consensus has emerged among managers that cost-benefit analysis is neither a panacea nor a sham. Cost-benefit analysis minimally provides a systematic way of thinking about the manifest and latent costs involved in establishing new programs. It also encourages more exhaustive examination of both the benefits and the unanticipated consequences of new programs.

During the 1970s, the interests of managers and students of organizational behavior shifted away from cost-benefit analysis to evaluation research, and the effects of this more recent focus are still evident. Today it is a rare program initiated by any government or private funding agency that does not automatically require and support an evaluation of its effectiveness. Given the incessant search for conceptual clarity in the social and policy sciences, we will no doubt see the emergence of new perspectives on how to assess the impact of programs operating in the context of complex organizations. For example, a common theme of goal clarification has now substantially affected organizational fiscal management, for it is widely recognized that programs clearly specifying their goals in advance are more amenable to systematic evaluation. Effective managers review proposals to initiate new programs by systematically considering whether the goals (benefits) to be gained can be viewed as worth the costs required. Estimating costs relative to benefits can assist a manager in distinguishing between relevant and irrelevant factors, a distinction of great value in any decision making.

Costs involved in obtaining computer support for library activities can be placed into four major categories:

1. hardware, including the central processing unit, peripheral devices, terminals, and telecommunications equipment to support networking;
2. software, including operating systems, utility packages, and applications programs.
3. personnel to design, implement, and operate the system; and
4. instructional activities to train both library staff and other members of the university community to use the new systems.

Hardware costs are the easiest to predict. They entail the comparatively fixed costs of equipment, supplies, and materials required by the automated systems, including computers, disks, tapes, cards, printout paper, and forms (for example, worksheets, claim notices, fine notices, and the like). Because automated systems make some manual files obsolete, the preprinted forms they require may be substantially fewer in number than those consumed by the manual systems they replace; nevertheless, the preparation of new forms frequently calls for a substantial initial outlay.

Both software and personnel costs are more difficult to predict than hardware costs, and this difficulty is related to whether the library decides to obtain computing services from a locally developed system or from the outside; for example, a commercial source or a nonprofit bibliographic cooperative. When a university library obtains a commercial system or participates in one of the cooperatives, the associated costs can be anticipated with a relative degree of certainty. One knows the costs of purchasing or leasing a turnkey system. One also knows the membership and transaction fees charged by a cooperative. Thus, yearly costs of operation can be forecast with reasonable accuracy. Of course, there are unexpected occurrences that may further increase costs above those initially projected, but it is relatively easy to estimate at least a range of cost increases. However, when a university library decides to develop a system in-house, cost estimates are very difficult to project. One may anticipate hardware costs accurately, but the software and personnel costs are another matter.

The time and money required for developing systems seem always to expand beyond initial expectations. System designers at the University of Chicago anticipated a two-year period to develop their library system. In fact, only after twelve years did the Chicago system include all its major components. Staff at Chicago had grossly underestimated the problems inherent in building and maintaining a system that shared a central computer with many other applications. The experience of underestimating the time and money needed to develop automated systems locally is certainly not unique to the University of Chicago; the same problems have been encountered by many university libraries. Wags frequently advise to increase carefully made estimates by a factor of ten to arrive at a realistic estimate of final expenditures for developing inhouse systems.

The fourth category of costs encompasses the resources required to instruct both the library staff and the user community in the operation of automated systems. To date little systematic effort has been exercised to instruct students and faculty in using library systems, primarily because most library automation has thus far focused on technical services. The Research Libraries Group has established a task force to work on the problem of instruction, for it is expected that member libraries will shortly provide public access to the on-line catalog. What costs arise from the necessary training of diverse user communities is still unclear.

Compared with estimating the costs of automated systems, measuring their benefits is a Herculian task. No university library has ever calculated definitively the monetary value of services delivered in manual systems; thus no base line exists from which to compare the benefits of automated systems. To be sure, many libraries have estimated the costs of cataloging a volume or of answering a reference question; but for the most part, such attempts have been piecemeal and have never been sustained. One must conclude that it is almost impossible now to place a dollar value on service improvements resulting from automation.

An interesting and potentially useful prototypical study was recently conducted at Washington State University by Joselyn Druschel.[3] The investigator compared the per-unit cost of book cataloging and end-processing in a manual system with the cost of performing these tasks using the Washington Library Network. The analysis revealed a 20-percent savings in the automated system, primarily in reduced staff costs. Unfortunately, the comparisons involve different time periods. However, the careful analysis of components of costs is exemplary.

University libraries' problems in measuring benefits are not unique. Indeed, all service organizations, whether profit or nonprofit, have difficulty in assigning quantitative values to their qualitative products. However, schools do estimate per-pupil expenditures, hospitals calculate average patient costs, and even prisons document their costs in maintaining an inmate for a given period. Although these and other measures do not account for variations in quality of education, medical care, or rehabilitation, they do shed light on selected aspects of services delivered.

As fiscal constraints become more stringent, increased demands for accountability in university libraries can be expected. Library managers are well advised to improve their procedures for systematically collecting time-series data on both the quantity and quality of the many services they deliver. Almost all libraries collect such routine data as number of volumes circulated, reference questions processed, volumes cataloged, volumes added, and the like. The Association of Research Libraries publishes some of these statistics annually for its members. But these are not very useful indicators of the quality of library services. Library managers might, for example, ask their user communities to assess the library's performance. There are definite risks involved in such an approach, but university administrators may find it necessary to implement user-survey procedures to meet future demand for accountability and to provide a foundation from which improvements in the quality of service delivery can be detected.

It would, of course, be impractical to attempt to assess the quality of each and every service performed by a university library. However, it is certainly possible to develop a sampling framework from which a subset of services could be assessed. Assessments could be derived from data collected from both the recipient and deliverer of the selected services. When collected over time these data could provide indications of change in the quality of library services, as perceived by both staff and users.

We are not able to quantify the effect on productivity of any automated system we examined in this study. Determining the relationship between a system and its output is complicated by the numerous other changes a unit undergoes that affect productivity. Some are brought on by the installation of the system, others are not. Summary data, the type of data a case study captures, reflect the net results of all changes. Ferreting from summary statistics the effect of one change, even a major change like the installation of a computer system, is impossible.

Let us illustrate this point by considering the data in table 5-1, which presents some measures of productivity for Chicago's cataloging department over several fiscal years. The 1973-1974 data represents the department's production level before LDMS was installed. The fiscal year 1976-1977 is a good starting point from which to examine the effects of the LDMS, for its was the first relatively stable year to follow the system's installation. Productivity for the years 1974-1975 and 1975-1976 was greatly affected by the turmoil of system installation and debugging and by a major reorganization of work and staff. The problems and distractions accompanying these events resulted in the unusually low output of about 30,000 titles in 1974-1975 and 32,000 in 1975-1976.

The number of books cataloged over each year appears in the first row of table 5-1. From these figures one might conclude that the LDMS undermined productivity. However, the drop in cataloged books was primarily due to a drop in the number of catalogers. As can be seen in the second row of data, the cataloging staff was cut by 20 percent between 1973-1974 and 1976-1977, a reduction owed primarily to budget constraints.

Because of the variation in staff size, a better statistic for summarizing productivity is provided by the data in the last row of the table. These data are calculated by dividing the number of cataloged books by the number of staff. They suggest that productivity fell slightly in 1976-1977 and rose significantly in 1977-1978. However, the connection between these production figures and the LDMS is also unclear.

In 1973-1974, 43 percent of the staff were professional librarians. In 1976-1977, this figure had dropped to 38 percent and by 1977-1978 to 26

Table 5-1
Catalog-Department Productivity—University of Chicago

	1973-1974	1976-1977	1977-1978
Titles cataloged	46,238	36,386	45,646
Staff	30	24	27
Professional	13	9	7
Clerical	17	15	20
Titles cataloged per staff member	1,540	1,520	1,690

percent. Because professional librarians primarily are involved in original cataloging and nonprofessionals in copy cataloging, one would expect per-employee production to go up as the level of expertise goes down. In fact, one might conclude from these data that in the later years, the department nearly matched and then exceeded a productivity level that was achieved in 1973 by relying more on Library of Congress cataloging, a situation forced by decreases in the number of professional librarians in the department and encouraged by the efficiencies that accompanied copy cataloging. In essence, the department managed to maintain and exceed the 1973 level by increasing their reliance on expertise supported outside the library. Because the LDMS is geared to exploit LC data, the system probably did play a significant role in the department's production level; however, the summary data of table 5-1 cannot be used to ascertain the magnitude of its role.

We conclude our discussion of costs and benefits by examining the cost of membership in a bibliographic cooperative. In addition to the obvious cost of membership fees, there are numerous hidden costs of network participation, including a decrease in library autonomy. Among the factors jeopardizing autonomy are the following. First, to use effectively the resources of a network, a library may have to change long-standing local practices. Second, libraries may have to adapt to system changes over which they have little or no control. Finally, decisions involving internal operations, decisions that once could be made unilaterally, may now require network approval.

Another hidden cost of network participation is staff time needed to integrate the benefits of membership into local procedures. This process may involve formal and informal training sessions, coordination meetings, or informational seminars. Participation may also necessitate major reorganization efforts prefaced by analyses of tasks and workflows.

The desire to minimize the effect of network membership on autonomy and internal procedures may motivate a library to become involved actively in network policy decisions. This involvement, in turn, is accompanied by costs. RLG, for example, regularly convenes a number of advisory committees. Participants must commit staff time to meeting preparation and attendance. Time must also be allocated for the dissemination of meeting information. In addition, the library must provide travel expenses and bear the disruptions to internal functioning that accompany the absence of key staff members.

Involvement of staff in interorganizational relationships may result in increasing the level of internal conflict in the library. Involvement may introduce staff to new perspectives and ideas they may wish to incorporate into their workplace. Interacting with comparable staff in other libraries introduces a librarian to new organizational features that can be compared to those of his or her own library. Failings and weaknesses that were once less evident may become highly visible. Finally, identification with external bodies may compete with allegiance to the librarian's own institution.

On the other hand, the costs of network membership must be weighed against benefits, most of which are also difficult, if not impossible, to quantify. The decreasing gain in resources relative to dollars invested has motivated the search for greater interdependencies between libraries. In addition to the obvious benefits of access to the bibliographic data and the holdings of other institutions, cooperation provides a mechanism for access to expertise in computing, for which the library pays only a portion of the cost. Also, private foundations and federal sources now favor support for cooperative arrangements as opposed to funding for individual libraries. Libraries in search of subsidies for their operations or for their development efforts are more likely to get them in the context of network membership.

A longer-range benefit of network participation may be a greater capacity for adapting to future change. Libraries that actively participate in the definition of specifications for bibliographic records and for the systems that disseminate them are able to influence development to the benefit of their operations. Libraries appear to be moving toward a national network. As in the case of bibliographic data, those libraries readying their internal operations to conform to trends and participating in shaping these trends will be able to adapt more readily to the national systems that evolve.

To review systematically the costs and benefits of automation, university librarians will need to supplement such quantitative data as they already have with assessments of quality. The institutions included in this study have not experienced substantial cost savings through staff reductions, and they seem increasingly to suspect that perhaps such cost savings in personnel may not soon materialize. This possibility, of course, raises questions about the validity of taking loans on future library budgets to offset the cost of automation. In our view, library managers will be requested in the near future to substantiate with empirical data their claims for the value of automation; and cost-benefit analysis focusing on the quality of services will soon become a topic of increasing salience in the lives of university librarians.

Physical Plant

That the introduction of automated activities into a university library frequently coincides with new construction or expansion of physical plant was clearly examplified in our case studies. At the University of Chicago and Northwestern University major innovations in automation were coincident with occupancy of a new main-library building. Undoubtedly, the implementation of automated systems is accompanied by major transformations in task assignments and workflow, changes that require a corresponding rearrangement of the physical layout of work space. The construction of a new physical plant facilitates such rearrangements, for the new space can be designed to accommodate automation, including both the equipment and the altered workflow. The design of the new buildings at Chicago and Northwestern clearly anticipated the introduction of their integrated automated systems. Perhaps the best-documented case of designing an academic library to accommodate automated systems can be found in Robert S. Taylor's description of the design of the library for Hampshire College in Massachusetts.[4]

The concurrent introduction of computer-aided systems and occupation of new space further compounds the already-complex issue of sorting out the effects of automation. In one sense, the two are interrelated causal factors, and it is exceedingly difficult, if not impossible, to single out their separate and unique effects.

The systematic study of the effect of space utilization on individual behavior and on an organization's effectiveness is a relatively new and as yet undeveloped field in the social sciences. Although the topic has been dealt with in a theoretical fashion by some of the earliest social scientists, including Max Weber, George Simmel, and Robert Park, the empirical investigation of the relationship between physical space and behavior patterns is still relatively rare. The classic study of space and behavior, conducted by Leon Festinger and his colleagues, demonstrated how physical proprinquity determined patterns of interpersonal interaction among the families of graduate students at the Massachusetts Institute of Technology.[5] Subsequently, the relationship of physical space to behavior has been studied by anthropologists,[6] psychologists,[7] and sociologists.[8] These investigations centered on identifying, in both work and residential settings, the relationship of proximity to patterns of interaction, productivity, morale, satisfaction, and self-concept. Such research has obvious implications for the design professions and calls for the creation of a new type of policy-oriented design research that examines intended and actual patterns of using physical space.

Our review of the research literature on academic libraries failed to uncover any systematic studies of the effects of automation upon the use of library space. Furthermore, given the limited resources available for this study, it was not possible in the case studies to collect sufficient data for analyzing the use of space. However, since two of the four libraries, Chicago and Northwestern, moved to new buildings as they embarked upon a major automation project, we can make several comments on salient issues for library administrators simultaneously creating new physical plants and planning for automation.

An obvious potential cost saving for a university library might be realized by sharing hardware with other campus computing activities, such as research, instruction, and administration. This sharing is exactly what was done at Stanford, Chicago, and Northwestern. However, since the time of our investigation, Northwestern has installed a computer dedicated solely to library activities, and Stanford now uses a machine that supports only RLIN activities. As the costs of computer hardware continue to decrease, it is unlikely that future cost savings will result from sharing computer facilities. Software, personnel, and training costs will account for most of the expenditures associated with library automation; and these costs are not reduced substantially by hardware sharing. Indeed, they may even be increased. Furthermore, the patterns of heavy-use periods for research, instruction, and administrative computing frequently conflict with the library's needs. Also, it is not uncommon in shared computing arrangements for the library to be given a lower priority than other campus users; for example, the administration.

It seems clear that libraries may find it most advantageous to obtain their own dedicated-computer system for automating major functions. A stand-alone system is much easier to interface with the regional and national library networks that provide access to the large bibliographic data bases. However, it would be prudent for the library to arrange to use the university computing center as a back-up system for its own stand-alone equipment. Also, as university libraries plan for new buildings or add to existing ones, they should design these facilities to accommodate enhancements to their systems, such as the additional telecommunications equipment for linkages to the networks of the bibliographic cooperatives.

For some time to come, reference materials will continue to be disseminated primarily in hardcopy form, but one can expect that reference materials increasingly will be published with computer-aided systems. Hence, machine-readable versions of reference materials will become more common and their distribution in this form more likely. University libraries should consider having public-access terminals widely distributed throughout the library and campus to provide easy access to on-line reference materials. Some of these materials would be stored locally, but more and more of these materials may be remotely located. In fact, many are already remotely available through the bibliographic-search services, which regularly add more reference tools to their offerings. One might expect that increasing portions of library budgets will be used to purchase access rights to materials rather than to obtain local ownership of copies.[9] Universities are always competing fiercely for the best students and faculty. Offering technology-based information resources to support instructional and research programs will constitute an important advantage in this competition.

In considering the distribution of these reference-terminal stations for public use, planners must anticipate how power lines will be laid throughout the building. New space should be designed so that terminals can be relocated as the collection expands and user needs change. In the recently completed addition to the main library at Stanford, hollow construction poles were used throughout the new facility to provide maximum flexibility to run cables to terminal stations. In addition, Stanford also foresaw that traditional library carrels would not be sufficiently large to house terminal stations. Libraries should plan to use forty-two- to forty-six-inch-wide carrels to allow space for terminals as well as writing areas. Librarians should also expect higher noise levels with the terminals and plan strategies for minimizing their disruptive effects.

The distribution of public-access terminals throughout a library and campus will alter the spatial configuration of reference services significantly. Supervision of terminal stations might most appropriately be given to reference librarians, and many reference activities might most effectively be conducted at the stations themselves. Undoubtedly, planning for increased instructional activity will be necessary to insure that both students and faculty learn to use on-line reference terminals effectively. Hands-on experience will be crucial. Projecting terminal screens onto larger monitors may also be useful for group-instruction sessions.

It is quite possible that automated bibliographic data bases—such as those maintained by OCLC, RLN, and WLN—promote interlibrary loans. Therefore, it may be prudent in designing any new physical plant to leave room for further growth in interlibrary borrowing. Given its increasing relationship to reference services, the interlibrary-loan section might effectively be located near the main reference unit.

Enhancements

The phrase *system enhancement* is used commonly to refer to an improvement in the software or hardware of a library's automated system. Librarians differ in how they apply the term. For some, a newly implemented computer system is an enhancement. Other librarians use the term more restrictively. For them, enhancements are system additions or modifications that result in improvements in the support of previously automated library functions, including the extension of that support to new library tasks within the functions. In this discussion, we use the latter and narrower definition. Corrections of programming errors or repairs to hardware generally are not considered enhancements, because they are attempts to attain or maintain previously defined system specifications.

The freedom a library has to initiate enhancements is determined by its degree of system ownership. Libraries maintaining custom-designed systems have more freedom than do those purchasing turnkey systems; and turnkey owners frequently have more freedom than do those subscribing to cooperatives. Enhancement requests from libraries in cooperatives must be considered within the context of the other libraries using the system. Commercial vendors enhance their products but, typically, not solely as a result of the particular needs of one consumer. Rather, enhancements are part of the overall development goals of a profit-seeking company. In some instances, libraries employ inhouse or hire outside expertise to modify turnkey configurations.

As with systems in general, the costs of enhancements can be viewed from several perspectives. First and most obvious are the direct financial burdens they pose. In fact, the fiscal considerations relevant for enhancements are conceptually identical, but usually smaller in scale, to those generally relevant for initial library automation. Enhancements may result in changes to library procedures both during and after their implementation. Staff may require training or retraining in system operation. Time may be required before procedures are carried out as efficiently as they were before the system change. Such incidents also represent financial costs to the library. However, in addition to the financial burden of system enhancements, there are also human factors that must be considered enhancement costs. For example, during the implementation, normal system operation may be disrupted for some areas of the library. The curtailment of activities, imposition of new tasks, or modification of routines resulting from disruptions may frustrate or irritate staff. Library users may be annoyed with the delays or deterioration in services that may accompany system disruption. Typically, there are several enhancements under consideration at any given time, and the decision to support one precludes action on another. Thus, another cost of an enhancement is inaction on other options.

Constraints on the resources that can be committed to enhancements force libraries to develop procedures for giving priority to enhancement recommendations. Formal procedures were in operation at Northwestern, Chicago, and Stanford. The University of Washington, which had at the time of our study only limited experience with automation, had not yet evolved formal procedures for initiating enhancements. We will briefly describe the procedures established at the other sites.

At all three sites, informal communication, as well as formal procedures, played a crucial role in the movement of enhancement suggestions through the library and the formulation of plans for implementation. Informal communication played an even more significant role at Stanford and Chicago, for it frequently was used to bypass rather elaborate bureaucratic structures. At all three sites, enhancement suggestions emanated from both systems and library staff using the system, especially those staff in departments where the system was an integral part of normal operating procedures.

Northwestern's priorities for action were determined by the systems staff, with the systems analyst assuming a major role in the decision making. For the most part, all requests coming from library staff to the systems office filtered through the systems analyst. The systems analyst decided which of these requests would be dealt with immediately and which could be delayed. She also decided which could most appropriately be addressed by changes in the software and which could be addressed by changes in operating procedures. A file was maintained by the analyst that allowed related system problems and ideas for system improvements to accumulate together. One system modification or system addition usually accommodated many of the compiled change requests.

A staff member in technical services, the coordinator of automation procedures, served as the conduit of requests from technical-services staff to the systems analyst. The coordinator prevented many day-to-day problems, solvable by procedural changes, from ever reaching the systems office. Some library staff chose to go directly to the systems analyst with their requests. However, action was seldom taken on staff requests without consulting the coordinator.

Modifications contemplated by the systems office were often brought to the attention of supervisors in areas affected by the changes. The systems analyst was responsible for disseminating this information, the intent of which was to assess problems that would result from the changes and to gather input from staff who would be operating the modified system.

The Chicago library formed a change-control committee to review and decide upon system-change requests in the mid-1970s. However, until the end of the decade there was little reason for the committee to function in a formal way. It seldom met and rarely reached closure on pending issues. Changes were for the most part negotiated informally, with systems staff and librarians often dealing directly with programmers. The time for programmers to work on most modifications was readily available, and the informal manner in which this time was allocated to tasks seemed to be working adequately.

However, diminishing financial support for Chicago's system forced the library to scrutinize how programming resources would be allocated. New priority-setting committees were introduced at the end of the decade, one concerned with the circulation system and the other with technical services. At the time of our study it was anticipated that the role of informal negotiation in initiating enhancements would decrease in importance. However, the informal networks that had directed much of the programming activity over the previous five years were now a part of the library's organization. Consequently it seemed likely that they would still significantly influence the direction of future system actions.

Before the establishment of RLIN, BALLOTS was used by over forty libraries. However, the Stanford computation center still regarded it as Stanford's system. The Stanford library was the major source of input concerning changes contemplated by the computation center; and the library's requests for system changes were granted higher priority than demands from other library users. When BALLOTS became RLIN, the organization operating and maintaining the system was restructured, and mechanisms for treating all network members more equitably evolved. Stanford now works within the new structure to initiate changes and communicate its concerns about changes proposed by RLIN staff or other RLG members. However, by virtue of its location, the Stanford library still has ready access to informal communication links that give it more influence over system development than other RLG members enjoy.

To make communications between member libraries and design and development staff easier, each RLG member is assigned a coordinator. System-modification requests are supposed to be sent from the libraries to their appropriate coordinator. At the time of this study, Stanford was having little luck getting action on its requests. Two reasons were offered for this: a considerable effort was underway to upgrade RLIN's networking capability, and few resources were available for other tasks. Furthermore, RLG's new members were now competing with Stanford for unallocated resources. In its striving for viability, RLG was devoting considerable attention to activities that would please recently acquired members and attract new members, sometimes at the expense of the needs of established members.

At the time of our study, two principal advisory committees furnished input for proposed system changes and developments. The committees were composed of representatives from each RLG member. Part of the responsibility of these groups was to react to documents prepared by RLIN staff describing contemplated system developments. The specifications for system changes or enhancements discussed in these documents were primarily the result of data gathered from member libraries concerning their needs and desires; and committee members reacted to the specifications in accordance with the requirements of the institutions they represented. The specifications finally acted upon by RLIN emerged from negotiations among the libraries and compromises between user needs and system capabilities.

Our review of the fiscal dimension has covered a wide field, including funding sources, the cost and benefit of automation, physical plant, and enhancements. We now turn to the final dimension from which automation will be viewed, personnel.

Notes

1. See for example Robert N. Anthony, *Planning and Control Systems;* Fremont J. Lyden and Ernest G. Miller, eds., *Planning, Program-*

ming, Budgeting; and for a discussion relevant to nonprofit organizations, Robert N. Anthony and Regina Herzlinger, *Management Control in Nonprofit Organizations.*

2. See for example Ida R. Hoos, *Systems Analysis in Public Policy.*

3. Joselyn Druschel, "Cost Analysis of an Automated and Manual Cataloging and Book Processing System," pp. 24–49.

4. Robert S. Taylor, *The Making of the Library.*

5. Leon S. Festinger, Stanley Schachter, and Kurt Back, *Social Pressure in Informal Groups.*

6. See Edward T. Hall, *The Hidden Dimension.*

7. See Roger Barker, *Ecological Psychology.*

8. See Robert Summer, *Personal Space;* Robert Gutman, ed., *People and Buildings;* and John Zeisel, *Sociology and Architectural Design.*

9. For a more complete discussion of this point, see F. Wilfred Lancaster, "The Future of Indexing and Abstracting Services," p. 184.

6 Personnel

Personnel is the fourth and last dimension considered in our comparative organizational studies of the effect of automation on university libraries. From this perspective, recruitment, hiring, placement, training, development, productivity, morale, and satisfaction are issues of concern. A particularly important element of the personnel dimension in a service organization is also the interaction between organizational members and clients. To be sure, not all components of the personnel dimension are significantly affected by automated activities; this chapter will stress those that are.

We begin the chapter with a summary of the social-science-research literature on leadership—and particularly on authoritarian-versus-democratic management styles. We then review the dilemma that arises when university-library directors must deal simultaneously with participatory management and the need for systems expertise. Next, we document changes in personnel management that can be associated with automation. We then examine the question of how different automated systems influence library-staff/user interactions. Although this discussion focuses primarily on reference services and circulation, it also touches upon collection development and some aspects of technical services. Finally, we turn our attention to preprofessional, continuing, and on-the-job training for professional staff in university libraries, a most important issue for the future of librarianship.

Leadership and Management

The effect of different styles of leadership on groups has long been a topic of investigation in social-science research.[1] The classic series of investigations on leadership styles was conducted by Kurt Lewin, Ronald Lippitt, and Ralph White, who examined three styles of leadership.[2] The first style was that of the *authoritarian* leader who determines all policies, procedures, and activities and maintains autonomy by remaining aloof from the group except when giving instructions. The second style, that of the *democratic* leader, allows all policies and activities to emerge from group discussions in which the leader takes an active part. In the third style, labeled *laissez-faire,* the leader permits the group membership to reach its own collective decisions without any active intervention from the leader. The findings demonstrated that groups having authoritarian leaders completed a larger number of tasks, but groups led by democratic leaders tended to produce products of higher quality. Generally, the laissez faire groups were somewhere in between on both the quantity and quality dimensions.

The Lewin, Lippitt, and White studies have been replicated in many different laboratory and organizational settings, and much effort has since been devoted to determining further the effects of leadership style, personality of managers, and situational characteristics on the quantity and quality of group performance. Extensive research over the years has shown that group behavior tends to be more effective when the members' expectations of the leader's behavior are accurate. In addition, when group members expect a democratic leader, this style is usually the most effective. However, in military or business organizations, where individuals are apt to expect supervision, the authoritarian style proves more effective.

The experiments of Lewin and his colleagues not only inspired much additional research but also prompted the interest in applied group dynamics that later gave rise to numerous programs of leadership training and organizational development and eventually led to sensitive training, encounter groups, and the like.[3] A direct consequence of the concern with social-psychological dimensions of leadership in organizations was the evolution of *participatory management,* a management mode that incorporates democratic styles of organizational leadership.

This kind of management encourages both a widespread and informed partnership in discussions and also the resolution of major policy questions by consensus. The Office of Management Studies of the Association of Research Libraries has conducted training programs for college and university libraries to encourage the use of participatory management. These group reviews and assessments of library operations are known as the Management Review and Analysis Program (MRAP). Despite its significant influence on many university-library operations, MRAP has not been uniformly accepted by university-library managers and is still thought of as a controversial approach.[4] Nevertheless, recent years have seen a general transition to more participatory management in university libraries.

Participatory management is closest to the democratic ideal when each member of the group has equal influence on final decisions. Still, it is obvious that total sharing is impossible to achieve in practice. When technical questions relating to automation are under consideration, it would be foolish to grant equal weight to each individual's input, because competence in automation is always unevenly distributed among staff. It is the library manager who must evaluate the technical competence of those sharing in technical decisions, but unfortunately the manager is often not sufficiently competent to make an informed judgment.

The problem of assessing the technical competence of staff is, of course, not unique to university libraries using computer-aided systems. Potential conflict between technical expertise and traditional supervisor-supervisee relationships in organizations is discussed extensively in the social-science literature.[5] Managers in many and varied organizations may be responsible for overseeing the performance of employees whose technical competence exceeds their own. Such managers must perforce develop alternative methods of monitoring technical performance. For example, they might rely upon outside experts for initial selection and periodic evaluation of technical personnel. They might also limit participation in management decision making to only those colleagues who have the requisite level of technological skills, thus adopting a modified or limited model of democratic management.

The tendency now is for library directors relying on participatory-management techniques to create new organizational structures, such as task forces and other special committees of library staff.[6] Some committees may be delegated authority to reach conclusions on policy; others may simply advise the library administration on policy. The working groups deal with an assortment of issues ranging from hiring new professional staff to determining the future of the card catalog. The use of committees both exploits staff know-how and permits all relevant internal perspectives to be brought to bear on policy decision making.

Library directors are with increasing frequency calling on external parties to participate in library management, a phenomenon that might be considered an outgrowth of the participatory-management ethos. A common practice is to convene an outside consulting committee, comprising persons competent in both university-library operations and computer-aided systems to support library activities. Another common pattern is to create an internal advisory committee drawn from the administration and faculty—representatives who have an interest in and knowledge of library activities as well as competence in automation. Some committees address a single decision and then are dissolved; others, usually called *advisory* or *visiting committees,* are established on a continuing basis with rotating memberships.

A visiting committee typically is convened once a year for one or two days. Written materials pertinent to current policy issues may be prepared by library staff and distributed to the committee members in advance of their visit. The committee might meet with staff or it might meet only with the library director. As needed, an executive session may be held. Some committees are established as advisory to the library director; others report to the university administration. Careful selection of committee members, clear instructions concerning expectations of their performance, and preparation of advance materials all contribute significantly to effective use of such outside committees. Frequently, visiting committees submit written reports after each visit. The distribution of these reports within the library and the university community can further increase the committee's contribution to effective library management.

It is not clear whether libraries will continue their move toward participatory management. Certainly the effectiveness of various management options depends on characteristics of the library and its host institutions.[7] Research and experience to date nevertheless suggest that university-library directors are well advised to construct systems that are neither completely authoritarian nor democratic. A combination of styles of leadership and organizational flexibility will be needed to cope with the constant change that now characterizes so many university-library settings.

Personnel Management

A university library makes use of three major groups of employees: professional librarians, support staff, and students. Within each group there are gradations of jobs, although jobs for students above the entrance level are rarely found. It is not uncommon for a university library to have twice as many support staff as professionals, and twice as many students as support staff. However, the number of students employed can be deceptive; seldom do students work more than part-time. Turnover within the ranks of support staff and students is exceedingly heavy. For example, at Washington and Stanford it was estimated to be around 40 percent per year.

The primary distinction between professionals and support staff is that professionals have graduate degrees in library science. However, considerable advanced training is found among the support staff, especially among those who are titled *library specialists*. Specialists often perform professional-level tasks but typically the range of tasks assigned to specialists is narrower than that assigned to professionals. For example, a specialist might spend all of his or her time converting the catalog records of other libraries into records compatible with local cataloging procedures; or a specialist with advanced training in art history might be assigned collection-development tasks and reference duties in this area. Specialists with language proficiencies may be asked to catalog materials written in foreign or classical languages.

A university community often provides the library with a more than adequate pool of talent to fill its support-staff positions. Among support staff may be found students working toward library degrees or doctoral candidates completing dissertations. One may find students who have interrupted their graduate training for various reasons or former students who have completed their undergraduate or graduate degrees but are reluctant to leave the community. Another class of library workers in support areas are spouses of students or faculty members. Frequently the spouses are college graduates who have few employment prospects beyond the library. Because the ranks of the support staff may include many highly trained persons performing functions approaching and sometimes equal to those of professional librarians, antagonism frequently develops between support staff and professionals.

The personnel-management policies of a university library must conform to those of the university. Conflicts may emerge in attempting to integrate the two structures. At the professional level, the conflict centers on whether librarians can be equated with faculty. At this point we might comment briefly on the popular discussion among many librarians concerning their professional status.[8] In our opinion the discussion can yield little that is useful and to the point. Professionalism is a dimension rather than a binary characteristic, and librarians devoting their energies to dealing with the many challenges that now confront them probably will achieve more that is professional if they avoid dissipating their efforts in debates over the nature or extent of their professional status.

At the support-staff level, the conflict centers on whether particular jobs are equivalent to comparable positions in other university departments, since highly specialized skills are required in many support-staff jobs. The difficulty of equating these skills with those of other university support staff has often resulted in creating unique job titles within the library.

The comparability of support staff inside and outside the library is complicated by the expanding use of computers by library personnel. The requirement to operate a terminal has in some libraries resulted in distinguishing support staff to such an extent that entire levels have been upgraded relative to their position within the total university structure. However, such upgradings often present difficulties for the library, which must maintain internal consistency between levels to insure that its employees are being treated equitably. Library personnel officers must determine whether use of a terminal signifies a meaningful elevation of skill level. In most cases, it is not clear whether a change in level of work really occurs.

As a terminal is integrated into operations, more and more ways are found to exploit its capabilities. Consequently, job specifications are changing continuously. This volatility has made the job of personnel officers still more difficult. A major responsibility of personnel is to justify to library staff differences in job levels, differences that are often difficult to substantiate even in stable environments.

Hiring practices for professionals, support staff, and students have also been affected by automation. Libraries now look for employees who are enthusiastic about the use of computers; for supervisory positions, they seek in addition experience in the use of computer-based systems. However, it is a curious fact that the demands of most supervisory positions make it impossible for supervisors to know all the ways in which staff employ computers. There are many technical aspects to system use, and procedures increase in complexity as system use continues. Supervisors often find it impossible to keep abreast of the so-called tricks their supervisees employ— while simultaneously attending to other supervisory duties, including co-ordinating the activities of their supervisees and the activities of their department with those of other departments. It is important to remember that effective supervisors must play key roles in facilitating the increased levels of within-unit and between-unit communication that accompany automation.

The investigators explored with many supervisors the qualifications they looked for when hiring new professional staff and found that extensive experience with computers was never mentioned as a prerequisite. Apparently, it was presumed that anyone coming from library school would have some experience with computers and could readily become familiar with the local system. However, the supervisors did stress qualifications that can be linked directly to the steadily increasing use of technology within the library community. Public-service librarians stressed the need for prospective employees to demonstrate sophisticated understanding of bibliographic records. Such sophistication would insure their ability to communicate intelligently with technical-services staff. Automation has decreased the distance between technical and public services, forcing public-service librarians to regard more closely the activities of their technical-service counterparts. A terminal at the reference desk now allows a reference librarian to follow the progress of an acquisition from the day an order request is submitted to the day the acquisition leaves cataloging for shelving, but this progress can only be monitored if a reference librarian understands how to read and interpret on-line bibliographic records.

Computer applications supporting technical services and circulation have only recently become accessible to public-service librarians, although, as has already been suggested, these applications are of enormous help in their work. Because the applications originally were intended to support non-public-service areas, public-service librarians had little to do with their design. The specific needs of public services were therefore overlooked— and today public-service librarians find themselves with an invaluable tool written in the language of technical services. However, they also now find themselves in a position to request enhancements to a system that will support their activities. Taking adequate advantage of the system requires knowledge of the operation of technical services; communicating fully their desires for future development efforts requires librarians to know how to address technical-service issues.

In the hiring of technical-service librarians, attention has turned to the ability to make appropriate decisions concerning the use of bibliographic data from external bodies, such as OCLC or the Library of Congress. The availability of external bibliographic support has the potential to make libraries less dependent on traditional cataloging skills. However, librarians must know how to evaluate these external sources, discriminate between acceptable and unacceptable data, integrate the use of external sources into the general operating procedures of the library, and merge data gathered from different data sources.

One justification for investing in automation is that the labor intensiveness of some library operations will decrease. Indeed, in some areas of the automated library, staff reductions have occurred. For example, in typing units involved in hardcopy-record creation, cutbacks have been achieved. Although libraries have invested in automation in part to decrease dependence on labor, most have avoided job terminations by depending on natural attrition and the movement of staff into other positions. This transition has not occurred without difficulty. A continuing problem for personnel offices within automating libraries is to find ways to absorb displaced persons.

Automation and the Library User

From the point of view of the user, a library's staff comprises two types of people: the visible and invisible. The visible are those in public services and circulation. The invisible are in technical services. Generally, the latter are concerned with acquiring and cataloging materials. Those in public services are mediators, assisting users who need help with the location tools maintained by technical services, such as the card catalog. A major task of technical services is to make material available for circulation. A major task of public services is to support the retrieval and use of that material.

Unquestionably, automation has made the activities of technical services much more visible to library staff outside of technical services. Still, it has done little to alter the traditional relationship, or perhaps more accurately, the nonrelationship, between the user and technical-services staff. Public-service librarians still link these parties. Thus in discussing automation's effect on library-staff/user interactions, we necessarily concentrate on circulation and reference.

Automation has greatly improved the efficiency of several user/library interactions in both circulation and reference services. For example, with automated circulation, users receive prompt notification of overdue books, the processing time of recalled items is shortened, and the time needed to charge-out or renew books is shortened. For material falling within the scope of on-line bibliographic data bases, user reference questions concerning holdings are answered more rapidly.

The increased efficiency of numerous interactions has in turn altered the nature of the user/library-staff relationship. The pace of manual book charging and searching of the public catalog and other bibliographic tools allows time for informal communication between library staff and users. On the other hand, the efficiencies of automated support for these activities discourage nonessential social contacts. To be sure, negative consequences may accompany the decrease in personal contact. Informal communication makes bearable an otherwise tedious job for many circulation attendants; it allows reference librarians to learn more about their user community; and for users, it fosters a perception of the library as a provider of services as opposed to a warehouser of information.

User/staff interactions in automated libraries are profoundly affected by system breakdowns. Computer failure has to be expected when working with automated systems. Since the charging of books cannot be halted when computer failures occur, automated circulation systems usually involve two systems, one supported by computer and the other by a manual back-up. The use of two systems can be irritating to users and frustrating for desk attendants if there is a great discrepancy in their efficiencies. When users and library staff become accustomed to one level of performance, coping sporadically with a system offering a lower level is difficult. Expectations for service resulting from automated systems are often unfulfilled in the manual environment, resulting in user and desk-attendant discontent. Furthermore optimal circulation policies may be different for automated systems than they are for manual systems. Manual circulation systems often appear even more awkward when they support policies established for an automated environment.

The traditional reference-librarian/user interaction concerning a bibliographic question is pursued by the reference librarian with the following strategy in mind. The librarian instructs the user to the point of self-sufficiency. Most often this instruction means directing a user to a reference tool, telling the user whether the library houses the needed material, or showing the user how to work with the card catalog or some other bibliographic data base. Some reference services provide additional assistance. For example, the University of Chicago library maintains a reference advisory service, in which librarians work with individual users on a specific research question. The reference librarian may compile a bibliography of reference tools or provide a personal tour of the library, focusing on resouces relevant to the user's research problem. At the time of the study, the University of Washington was about to initiate a service in which users could request subject bibliographies that reference librarians would compile from citations within the WLN data base.

Perhaps the most well-known reference service that goes beyond the traditional involves the commercially available machine-readable data bases. When undertaking an on-line search, the librarian becomes substantively involved in the client's problem, spending considerably more time with a patron than is spent in a traditional reference-desk interaction. Relative to the traditional context, the interaction is more formal and structured. An appointment is made and forms have to be completed. The librarian/user interaction focuses on the scope of the search and the identification of retrieval terms.

Libraries have found it necessary to charge for on-line search services, recovering at least part of their cost. As noted above, many librarians believe that all library services should be free, because those that charge fees are ultimately available only to the affluent. Because the additional time needed for on-line searching may limit the time available to support traditional reference services, many libraries deliberately limit search activities. Librarians who view on-line services as elitist are particularly supportive of this curtailment. Other librarians argue that, relative to the service provided by an on-line search, students and faculty can afford to undertake a search. Furthermore, the expected growth in the use of search services will justify expanding reference staffs, an outcome that would benefit all library users.

Increasingly, users are requesting from libraries material in nontraditional formats. For example, faculty and graduate students in engineering seek with more frequency technical reports, conference papers, preprints, and other fugitive documents. The commercial indexing services are largely responsible for the increased awareness of the existence of such documents. Not only are these materials seldom available inhouse, but they are also almost impossible to retrieve through standard interlibrary-loan channels. Reference librarians, particularly in the sciences, are finding it necessary to build informal interlibrary-loan networks, including special librarians in research institutes and industry, to fulfill user demand for the fugitive literature.

Selective dissemination services are now offered by some university libraries, particularly by branch units serving the sciences. These services are often based on alerting systems maintained by the data-base vendors. Alternatively, the library can acquire directly the machine-readable tapes of data bases; for example, chemical abstracts.

Some large academic departments have bypassed the library as an agent to provide selective dissemination services, supporting with departmental funds the acquisition of the necessary machine-readable tapes and the maintenance of staff to operate the system. This departmental initiative is one example of a more general phenomenon: academic libraries are finding it more and more difficult to keep up with the information needs of their users and the technologies that facilitate information transfer. The availability of data in machine-readable form and efficient systems for their analysis and dissemination have resulted in a proliferation of organizations that will retrieve subsets of the data on request, sometimes free of charge but most often for a fee. Examples include SPIRES, which maintains machine-readable citations of physics preprints, technical reports, and journal publications; the Current Research Information System (CRIS), a service supported by the Department of Agriculture that maintains on-line data of the research activities of the nation's agriculture stations; and centers located across the nation that contract commercial on-line search services and, in turn, provide their services to anyone wishing to pay the necessary fees.

As tools to answer reference questions, terminals linking the reference desk to the library's on-line bibliographic records have become invaluable to reference librarians. With the terminals, librarians can answer questions they could only answer with difficulty before. In fact, during weekend and evening hours, when the reference desk is operating but technical services are closed, the terminal allows reference librarians to deal with questions that would otherwise be impossible to answer because of the lack of access to technical-service files. However, even during normal working hours terminal data are often the only source of information that can answer a user's query. For example, Northwestern has stopped updating manual records documenting serials holdings. Instead, holdings are recorded in Northwestern's on-line serials support system. Thus, reference librarians must turn to the on-line system for holding information.

Both reference librarians and library users quickly come to depend on the terminal when it is available in the reference area. The typical bibliographic question concerns holdings. Although on-line holdings information may not be comprehensive, often the reference librarian's first reaction is to check the terminal because it is so easy to do so. If the needed records are found, the user's question is answered immediately. If not, the search has added little time to the user/reference-librarian interaction. For the user, the terminal has become a convenient link to materials in process. In many cases, a user has more points of access to a book-in-process via the terminal than through the public catalog. Although temporary cards are available for books-in-process, they are filed only under main entry and kept in this limited state of access until full cataloging is completed, which may take months and perhaps even years.

The terminal has facilitated the movement of user-requested books through technical services. Many libraries rush material through processing if it has been specifically requested. The terminal can alert a user to the fact that the library has ordered the material and that it now exists in some form somewhere in technical services. A reference librarian can then tell the user that the simple act of requesting the material will quicken its pace through processing.

Faculty attitudes toward automation in their libraries vary. Some are greatly concerned that money spent on automation is money taken from collection development. In fact, at one of the institutions visited, a faculty library advisory board several years ago established priorities for the allocation of library resources. The highest priority was given to the acquisition of materials. Processing of materials was second in importance, and reference services followed in third place. The advisory committee established these priorities in response to concern over the effect of automation costs on the library budget.

Ironically, the introduction of computers in university libraries may make it more difficult for users to find materials they seek, making them more dependent on reference librarians. Libraries are moving toward on-line catalogs. Users will eventually have two catalogs to cope with, the manual file of older acquisitions and the on-line file documenting newer acquisitions. Users will have to learn which of the catalogs is likely to contain the data of interest. Furthermore, the conventions of each catalog will probably be different, with the on-line file reflecting the most up-to-date standards. This disparity may be a great and continuing source of confusion for catalog users.

The present organization of bibliographic instruction appears inadequate to train users to handle the increasing complexity of library retrieval systems. To ignore user difficulties would be inconsistent with automation's objective of improving library services. Improvement in bibliographic instruction, probably leading to an expansion of public services, seems the only alternative. It is somewhat ironic that, as a result of technology, public services may expand. Automation, which many anticipate will lead to cutbacks in the personnel needs of technical services, may in turn force libraries to increase their support for public services.

Professional Training

Whenever a new technology and its accompanying body of expert knowledge are introduced into an organization, managers must review the adequacy of training programs that make possible the utilization of that new technology. All organizations have procedures for training members in accomplishing necessary tasks. In many instances, the methods are informal, consisting merely of on-the-job instruction by more experienced colleagues. As present-day organizations adopt new and more complex technologies, training requirements become more extensive and complex. As new systems for the storage, retrieval, and transfer of information multiply, appropriate entry-level and continuing-education programs take on new importance. The rapid spread of innovations, such as microcomputers, increases the rate at which existing training programs must be updated and new ones introduced.

Before they can even be hired by an organization for specific task assignments, many individuals must spend long periods, often years, in training programs in colleges, graduate programs, or technical and vocational schools. This fact is true for most professions. Medical practitioners, for example, are usually required to complete four years of post baccalaureate academic training and then several years of practical internships or residencies before they are licensed to practice. Librarians must obtain a graduate library degree, typically awarded after a one-year training program—but increasingly two-year graduate programs are being required by library schools.

In recent years, the rate of technological advance in the practice of many professions has given rise to expanding requirements for continuing education. Thus, several medical specialties now require practicing physicians to take additional training periodically and to pass certifying examinations to retain their licenses. Regardless of legal or formal requirements for continuing education in a profession, the level of competence attained in most preprofessional training is obviously no longer adequate to maintain a practitioner's competence throughout a career that may span forty years. Social change occurs at such a rapid rate that preprofessional training programs must be complemented with continuing-education, career-development, on-the-job-training, and proficiency-certification programs. It is within the context of burgeoning training requirements and programs that we examine the effect of automation on the education of university librarians.

As we mentioned above, debates about comparative professional status are, in general, nonproductive. However, a consideration of how other professions manage entry-level training, career development, and continuing education can be most illuminating. Over the years, each profession has developed its unique procedures for instructional programs, maintenance of professional competence, and facilitation of career transitions. Thus, the medical profession requires residencies that result in intensive clinical experience; it encourages affiliations with group practices and hospitals that provide mechanisms for peer supervision and performance monitoring. The use of clerkships and junior partnerships accomplishes a similar form of supervision and on-the-job training in the legal profession.

Librarians might examine these and other models with a view toward possible adaptation to their field. Some librarians, however, foresee unjustified and invidious comparisons that will arise from such scrutiny. Granted that the situation is a sensitive one, an analysis of the procedures and techniques used in other fields for preprofessional, continuing, and on-the-job training might nevertheless prove useful. Continuing-education programs in law, medicine, and business administration are numerous and well attended; they are coordinated by graduate schools and professional associations. Such coordination is patently not yet the case in the profession of librarianship, which still suffers from insufficient opportunities for continuing educational activities.

In our interviews with over two-hundred librarians in this study and over three-hundred academic librarians in an earlier study of collection-development policies and practices,[9] we routinely asked interviewees to provide a brief assessment of their training in graduate library-school programs. With very few exceptions, informants gave strongly negative assessments of their library-school experience. Most felt that the training programs lacked both intellectual strength and pertinence to subsequent professional practice. We also routinely asked library administrators to assess the quality of training received by those the library recently had hired directly from a graduate-training program. Again, with very few exceptions, administrators decried the weak training and claimed that immediate corrective action had been required to bring the new employees to a minimum level of performance. Such general disparagement of the quality of library education by more than five-hundred librarians in eleven college and university libraries reveals the level of dissatisfaction that now exists among practicing professionals regarding graduate library training.

The criticisms, of course, include a variety of issues. One must, however, note that none of those interviewed complained about the training received in the use of automated systems. Most interviewees thought that previous training or experience in the use of automated systems was not an important qualification for entry-level professional positions in a university library. The most desirable characteristic uniformly required was general intelligence, the assumption being that intelligence best qualified candidates to learn rapidly whatever might be necessary in the automation area. The consensus was that such training was just as effectively accomplished on the job as in the library school.

This perception may, however, pose a problem for university libraries because it reflects only a short-range perspective. It may well be that over the next few years requirements for technical competence will be fairly limited. At present, for example, it may be the case that librarians should be able to access on-line bibliographic-data files and operate the commercial search services. However, this minimum will remain adequate only if one assumes that the kinds of systems university libraries employ will not change. This assumption is surely unwarranted given the rate of technological change in libraries during the past decade.

A useful comparison can be made here with the experiences of social scientists. In the early 1960s, they began to use computers, primarily for data processing and statistical analyses. Shortly after, programs were produced and made available through computing centers to accomplish these tasks. When faculty began providing instruction on the use of computers for data manipulation, they for the most part taught graduate students how to use the locally available programs. The instruction was either integrated into existing methods courses or offered as special noncredit short courses through the department or university computing center.

Within a few years, however, it became clear that this method of instruction was not totally adequate. The graduate students very quickly learned how to use the new computer programs, and they became heavily dependent upon them. However, when they moved to new locations to take a first teaching or research position, they were exposed to another set of local programs and procedures. The previous instruction did not provide a sufficient base to allow them to transfer their knowledge. In many instances, they became totally incapacitated. It also became clear that computers were being used almost exclusively to accomplish methodologies that had existed long before the introduction of computers and that social-science research was not taking advantage of the new kinds of numerical and symbol manipulation afforded by computers.

Consequently, a number of graduate-training centers in the social sciences revised their programs to include courses that provided a basic introduction to the design and logic of computers, the kind of course that was by then routinely offered to entering students in computer science and electrical engineering. The results of this instruction have been much more satisfactory. Social scientists exposed to these basic courses are now able to use the computer to support a variety of research methods; for example, simulation, modeling, and network and content analysis.

Training programs for librarians in automation are now going through a similar phase. The training offered in most graduate schools of library science is limited to operating currently available systems. One should, of course, seek to know exactly how much librarians need learn about computers; and library-school faculty should exercise leadership in a thorough review of this issue. Too many have simply assumed that it is sufficient to teach students how to use present systems.

It is possible that the question of adequate training in computers for librarians is a temporary one. Increasingly, students from elementary school through graduate school are receiving greater exposure to the use of computers. It may well be that within several decades all student entering graduate library schools will have sophisticated understanding of and competence in the use of computers. Thus, the question of computer competence among librarians may eventually disappear; but how long it will take to reach that point cannot now be forecast accurately.

A more general question may appropriately be posed here: should librarians become masters of all technologies relevant to information transfer, including satellite transmission and video disks as well as computers? Our interview data suggest that university librarians believe they have problems enough just in coping with computer-aided systems that deliver traditional library services; they do not wish to tackle new services and technologies. However, unless university librarians master the new technologies, they may be bypassed by those that emerge to manage information-transfer systems of the future.

Notes

1. For an excellent review of this literature, see Ralph M. Stogdill, ed., *Handbook of Leadership*.

2. Kurt Lewin, Ronald Lippitt, and Ralph K. White, "Patterns of Aggressive Behavior in Experimentally Controlled 'Social Climates,'" pp. 271–299.

3. See for example Rensis Likert, *New Patterns of Management*; and Warren G. Bennis, *Changing Organizations*.

4. See Michael K. Buckland, ed., "The Management Review and Analysis Program"; and Edward R. Johnson and Stuart H. Mann, *Organization Development for Academic Libraries*.

5. See Talcott Parsons's extended footnote on the distinction between authority derived from incumbency versus competence in A.M. Henderson and Talcott Parsons, eds., *Max Weber*; Alvin W. Gouldner, *Patterns of Industrial Bureaucracy*; and Jerold Hage, *Communication and Organization Control*.

6. See for example Louis Kaplan, "The Literature of Participation," pp. 473–479.

7. For a discussion of some of these characteristics see Richard Eggleton, "Academic Libraries, Participative Management, and Risky Shift," pp. 96–101.

8. See William J. Goode, "The Theoretical Limits of Professionalization," pp. 266–315; and William James Reeves, *Librarians as Professionals*.

9. Hugh F. Cline and Loraine T. Sinnott, *Building Library Collections*.

7 Conclusion

We venture now beyond the implications of our data to speculate on inter-related issues pertinent to formulating policy on planning, operating, and financing automated library activities. We realize that four case studies are not an adequate base for generalizing to all university libraries; hence, we are reluctant to draw conclusions or make recommendations. Not only are our empirical data inadequate for conclusions, but we lack also the requisite background or experience to make recommendations. We nevertheless believe that our perspective as informed outsiders gives us insights that may be useful to those entrusted with the welfare of libraries. Thus we feel compelled to go beyond our data. We hope to be provocative and to encourage systematic review of vital matters affecting how university libraries collect, store, retrieve, and facilitate the use of their holdings.

Management Issues

Automation within the information-processing community has introduced several new organizational forms. Libraries now deal with data-base vendors; for example, Lockheed; book vendors connected to them by computer terminals; for example, Brodart; vendors of computer systems, some maintaining communication links to libraries after system implementation; for example, Gaylord; and library networks that have grown out of or been modified by new technologies; for example, RLG, WLN, and OCLC. The introduction of new organizational forms brings with it an increase in the number of links a library may have to other organizations. The modification of old forms is accompanied by changes in established relationships. When there are new or changed relationships, a library must contend with defining new interorganizational ties, the maintenance of which may blur previously defined organizational boundaries.

Unquestionably, new relationships result in staff members' informal or formal assumption of boundary-spanning roles to maintain the required links. Boundary-spanning roles are common within libraries. Bibliographers, for example, are linked to faculty, acquisitions staff to book vendors, technical-service staff to the Library of Congress, and reference staff

169

to other libraries. The new organizational forms consequent upon automation have impelled still more staff into roles linking a library to its environment. Those who play boundary-spanning roles become the primary source of information about their particular environmental area. They are also largely responsible for a library's visibility within the information community.

As the environment to which a library is linked becomes more complex, and the complexity of the library itself increases, the need increases to designate formally boundary-spanning personnel. The time and effort required to collect external information and facilitate its transfer to appropriate components within the library grow with the complexity of the environment. This fact is true, too, for the time and effort required to monitor the library's needs and to convey them appropriately to the environment.

Automation is changing the library community at such a rate that trends are difficult to unravel. This flux gives library staff maintaining links to organizational entities associated with automation considerable autonomy and power. Information is filtered through and interpreted by boundary spanners who exert a large degee of control over who receives information within the organization. Among library staff, boundary spanners are most able to influence future developments, and their capacity to insure that developments are consistent with the interests of the library adds further to their status.

Relationships with other organizations provide the bridge for external influences to penetrate internal operations. New ideas and perspectives are introduced by boundary spanners. Sometimes the information may alter long-established departmental practices and interdepartmental relationships. Libraries that join networks, for example, may sacrifice autonomy in internal policies and procedures to participate fully in the benefits of network membership.

It frequently occurs that new interorganizational relationships are accompanied by growth in the number of groups to which a library is accountable. All university libraries are of course accountable to the faculty and students they serve as well as to their institutional administrators; universities or colleges in state systems are furthermore accountable to state administrators. When libraries join networks, however, they find still other groups to contend with—the libraries within the network and the network administrators.

The groups to which libraries are accountable have expectations of library behavior, and often these multifarious expectations are incompatible, particularly in the light of the expectations of the primary constituents, faculty and students. Faculty and students expect that the materials they need can be acquired through the library. Institutional administrators, however, expect libraries to operate within the constraints of diminishing purchasing power. Statewide administrators may expect campus libraries to specialize in particular areas of collection development. Network members may expect improved access for their users to other member holdings. Network administrators may expect acceptance of technical-processing support that favors the processing of traditional- rather than nontraditional-material formats.

The emergence of new or modified organizational forms attributable to automation will continue. Changes in technology will be accompanied by further environmental changes. And even if the present state of technology were to be frozen, the environment would continue to change. For example, it is within the capacity of present technology to build far-more-encompassing nationwide networks to support various library activities, and considerable pressure is being applied within the library community to do so.

Thus, library managers can expect to deal with a changing environment for the indefinite future. New possibilities for relationships will be born, as will the need for their evaluation. Libraries aspiring to positions of leadership will have to monitor continually a turbulent environment to insure that external developments can be integrated readily into local operations. Libraries actively participating in external developments will perforce be coping with the many internal changes that result from maintaining such relationships. In previous chapters we have pointed out that library automation entails continuing adaptations in policy and procedure because of system modifications or enhancements. These changes may, in fact, be trivial when compared to the alterations in library structure and function arising from a library's response to transformations in its environment.

Computer applications within libraries often end in more closely connecting structures and activities throughout the organization. This result occurs particularly with integrated library systems. Unit interdependence means that adaptations made by one will influence the policies and procedures of another. In the traditional manual library, departments had considerably more freedom to make changes without disturbing operations elsewhere.

The last management issue to be discussed here concerns a short-term phenomenon; namely, the present nature of competition among libraries. The competition is significant because it involves basic philosophical approaches to future developments in library automation. Interlibrary vying has traditionally occurred at the level of the host institution. That is, university libraries have not directly competed with one another; rather, the rivalry has been that of the universities and it has centered on collection strength. However, particularly in the present-day contest for external funding, the competition now more directly exists among libraries, library networks, and the bibliographic cooperatives, OCLC, RLG, and WLN.

The focus of community attention currently appears to be on the conflict between RLG and OCLC, whose philosophical positions are quite different. OCLC maintains a system designed to be accessible to all libraries; RLIN aspires to be a tool that supports research libraries. Characteristics of the systems reflect these differing positions. Many within the library community believe that one organization will flourish to the detriment of the other. From the point of view of university libraries, especially public institutions, the approach of RLG is elitist but is consistent with RLG's interest in developing an effective tool to support costly programs like collection development, preservation, and technical processing. The so-called populist view of OCLC appears to be consistent with the desire of public institutions to inform local libraries of their holdings for the purpose of resource sharing. Over the next few years, the activities of library managers within both academic and public libraries will determine whether both points of view, and the organizational forms in which they are manifested, can survive.

Organizational Change

In contrast to 1980, the university library of 1960 was a relatively stable organization. There were, of course, important changes occurring in the sixties. Acquisition rates and budgets were increasing; libraries were running short of professional staff; backlogs in cataloging were accumulating; libraries were experimenting with new plans for acquiring materials; and bibliographers were establishing acquisitions and exchange plans with foreign institutions. However these kinds of changes are minor in comparison to the alterations in structure and communication patterns that characterize today's university library.

University libraries are being pummeled by profound and undoubtedly permanent changes. For example, the distinction between public and technical services appears to be eroding; communications within the library and with outside organizations are taking on new dimensions; and new demands are being placed on professional staff. These shifts and turns, moreover, are not one-time modifications to which libraries subsequently adjust, quickly rebounding to the status quo. Rather, automation apparently introduces continuous change; relentless revision is now inexorably an attribute of the university library.

Automated systems seldom reach states of sustained stability; hence, the permanence of organizational revision. Equipment becomes outmoded and needs to be upgraded. As use increases, demand eventually exceeds supply. Upgrading equipment generates a need to develop new software to capitalize on the hardware investment. A cycle of hardware and software acquisition, saturation, and replacement is established.

University libraries must develop procedures and structures to minimize the disruptions in their operations that inevitably accompany system changes. Some modifications or enhancements to systems result in more radical transformations to the organization than do others. However, the era in which university-library managers could readily anticipate alternating periods of organizational turbulence and calm appears to be at an end, at least for the foreseeable future.

The effect of automation on organizational stability is not, however, totally a negative one. For example, policy and procedural changes costly to introduce in manual environments are more affordable in automated environments. New cataloging rules or conventions can be incorporated efficiently into on-line cataloging systems. Such changes are considerably more difficult to implement in manual systems, and they are often ignored entirely because of their cost. Changes in cataloging procedures will become commonplace and routine because they are so readily accomplished with automated systems.

Development of new technologies relevant to information transfer is bound to continue at an increasing rate in the decades ahead. One has only to look at the recent history and projections of developments in the microelectronics industry to realize that this industry will be one of rapid growth. It seems certain that smaller and less-expensive microcomputers will proliferate. University libraries will begin to employ these machines for stand-alone computing, complementing their access to larger computers available through telecommunications networks. How this configuration of centralized and distributed computing can be used most effectively in libraries remains to be seen. But that distributed computing will take hold is now an established fact.

New capacities will be developed to access information in more effective ways. Subject access will be greatly improved and access to materials at lower levels of organization, such as to articles within journals, will be developed. In addition, university libraries will begin to collect and make available to users new types of materials in machine-readable form. The acquisition of these materials will present new challenges and new ways to use the ever-expanding capacities of information storage, retrieval, and transfer systems.

We are, however, not confident that university librarians fully recognize that the adoption of automated systems has moved libraries into an environment of continuous change. If libraries are to maintain their effectiveness, this fact must be appreciated fully by practitioners and by those who provide training for university librarians.

Future Organization

It appears the organization of university libraries is undergoing fundamental transformation. We speculated earlier on the possibility that libraries will adopt matrix management. This transformation may occur intitially in combination with the traditional functional organization, but we also anticipate that there may be basic modifications in the functional organization as well. As evidence, we cite the many moves in this direction already discernible in university-library structure.

We have speculated previously that systems departments may be dismantled, no longer to function as separate units within university libraries. We anticipate further change when item selectors have ready access to terminals for their collection-development activities. At present, most item selectors manually prepare order slips, which are then forwarded to the acquisitions department for preorder searching. Acquisitions staff are responsible for actually placing orders. Enhancements to automated-system capabilities will eventually allow item selectors to initiate purchase orders directly. When all item selectors have ready access to terminals for searching on-line catalogs and intitating orders, many tasks currently assigned to the acquisitions department will be accomplished by selectors.

The university libraries included in our study disclose that between 60 and 80 percent of all their current cataloging is accomplished through the automated systems they employ. This coverage is likely to increase, but it is unlikely that original cataloging will ever completely disappear in university libraries. By their very nature, university libraries must acquire material that are unique and therefore require original cataloging by professional librarians. However, it is evident that this activity will come to represent a smaller portion of all cataloging as shared acquisitions programs and the sharing of bibliographic data among research libraries become more extensive.

Given that university libraries will soon find the workload of acquisitions and original-cataloging units greatly diminished, it would make sense for managers to begin planning for the reorganization of their libraries. One likely approach might be to group library staff according to the fields they serve: natural sciences, social sciences, or humanities. Within each of these major clusters, there could then be further division by disciplines. Professional librarians would be assigned to specific substantive areas and have overall responsibility for collection management and use, including item selection, ordering, and cataloging. Librarians would also devote a substantial portion of their time to delivering reference services to scholars using those portions of the collections for which they have responsibility.

Some evidence exists that changes consistent with this kind of reorganization have already occurred. At the University of Washington, for example, those units traditionally assigned to technical-services divisions are now part of what is called *bibliographic control,* and unit staff members are encouraged to recognize that they are indeed performing public services. In many university libraries, public services are already organized substantively. Automation is causing increased interaction between public- and technical-service units. Many library managers interviewed during this study reported that public services are greatly improved when reference librarians increase their familiarity with technical-service operations. In some instances, reference librarians are routed books for original cataloging so as to sharpen their skill in locating material. That a number of former original catalogers are now performing public-service functions is further evidence that the distinction between public and technical services is eroding.

If libraries are reorganized along substantive dimensions, what would become of units dealing with particular formats of materials; that is, with government documents and microforms? In the past, it was very sensible to separate these units organizationally because of the unique problems involved in acquiring, cataloging, and retrieving the formats. However, if the remainder of the library were to be organized substantively, it might make better sense to distribute tasks associated with documents and microforms as well. This shift would require more librarians to gain expertise in handling these formats. The growth in university-library holdings of both these formats has increased dramatically in recent decades. One may expect this trend to continue. Materials available in these formats will undoubtedly increase in importance for future user communities.

University libraries may have to make special provisions for users who need materials that cross disciplines. Interdisciplinary research and instructional programs within one of the major groupings of humanities, social sciences, or natural sciences may not pose as serious problems as those that cross the major groupings. For example, users interested in environmental studies or physiological psychology would draw materials from both the natural and social sciences. Universities that develop interdisciplinary programs may find it necessary to hire librarians whose bibliographic and substantive knowledge spans the disciplines encompassed by the programs.

This kind of division of labor in university libraries raises additional questions about career patterns for academic librarians. Librarians would become subject specialists in particular areas, and it would be unlikely that a librarian in the course of one career would cover more than one field, or at least more than one major discipline grouping. What then would be the appropriate background for library administrators? A librarian who specialized in a grouping of social sciences could eventually be the head of the social-science division of the library. But does this position provide adequate experience for higher-level management positions within the library?

Many students of and practitioners in organizations believe that top-level managers can readily transfer from one type of organization to another; that is, someone who is the chief executive officer of an oil company may function just as well if transferred to the same position in an electronics

firm or government agency. It may well be that the executive leadership
needed for university libraries is similar to that needed for computing
centers or other academic administrative positions. Certainly, ample prece-
dent exists for nonlibrarians serving as directors of university libraries. Such
an idea, of course, does not please professional librarians who prefer to
guard their exclusive right to attain the highest position within a library.
Nevertheless, from the perspective of the university administration, the goal
is to provide library services to the host institution not to protect the interests of one particular set of employees within the university.

We are not suggesting that university libraries be administered by nonlibrarians; we are simply pointing out that university libraries very surely
will undergo extensive changes in organizational structure. The question is
therefore raised as to who will be best qualified to direct these radically
different organizations—a question without an unambiguous answer at this
time.

Bibliography

Anthony, Robert N. *Planning and Control Systems: A Framework for Analysis.* Boston: Harvard Business School, 1965.

Anthony, Robert N., and Regina Herzlinger. *Management Control in Nonprofit Organizations.* Homewood, Ill.: Richard D. Irwin, Inc., 1975.

Bahr, Alice H. *Automated Circulation Systems, 1979–80.* 2d ed. White Plains, N.Y.: Knowledge Industry Publications, 1979.

Barker, Roger. *Ecological Psychology.* Palo Alto: Stanford University Press, 1968.

Barnard, Chester I. *The Functions of the Executive.* Cambridge, Mass.: Harvard University Press, 1958.

Bennis, Warren G. *Changing Organizations.* New York: McGraw-Hill, 1966.

Brewer, Annie M., ed. *Dictionaries, Encyclopedias, and Other Word-Related Books, 1966–1974.* Detroit: Gale Research Company, 1975.

Buckland, Michael K., ed. "The Management Review and Analysis Program: A Symposium." *The Journal of Academic Librarianship* 1 (1976): 4–14.

Cline, Hugh F., and Loraine T. Sinnott. *Building Library Collections: Policies and Practices in Academic Libraries.* Lexington, Mass.: D.C. Heath and Co., Lexington Books, 1981.

Council on Library Resources, Inc. *A National Periodicals Center Technical Development Plan,* 1978.

DeGennaro, Richard. "Libraries and Networks in Transition: Problems and Prospects for the 1980s." *Library Journal* 106 (1981):1045–1049.

Dowell, Arlene T. "A Five-Year Projection of the Impact of the Rules for Form of Heading in the Anglo-American Cataloging Rules, 2nd Edition, upon Selected Academic Library Catalogs." Ph.D. dissertation, University of North Carolina, Chapel Hill, 1981.

Druschel, Joselyn. "Cost Analysis of an Automated and Manual Cataloging and Book Processing System." *Journal of Library Automation* 14 (1981):24–49.

Eggleton, Richard. "Academic Libraries, Participative Management, and Risky Shift." In *New Horizons for Academic Libraries,* edited by Robert D. Stueart and Richard D. Johnson. New York: K.G. Saur, 1979.

Fasana, Paul J. "The Collaborative Library Systems Development Project: A Mechanism for Inter-university Cooperation." In *Collaborative Library Systems Development,* edited by Paul J. Fasana and Allen Veaner. Cambridge, Mass.: MIT Press, 1971a.

Fasana, Paul J. "The Columbia Experience." In *Collaborative Library*

Systems Development, edited by Paul J. Fasana and Allen Veaner. Cambridge, Mass.: MIT Press, 1971b.

Festinger, Leon S.; Schachter, S.; and Back, K. *Social Pressure in Informal Groups.* New York: Harper, 1950.

Goode, William J. "The Theoretical Limits of Professionalization." In *The Semi-Professions and Their Organization: Teachers, Nurses, Social Workers,* edited by Amitai Etzioni. New York: Free Press, 1969.

Goodman, Paul S., ed. *Change in Organizations.* San Francisco: Jossey-Bass, 1982.

Goodwin, C.A. *The Library of Congress.* New York: Praeger, 1974.

Gouldner, Alvin W. *Patterns of Industrial Bureaucracy.* New York: Free Press, 1954.

Gutman, Robert, ed. *People and Buildings.* New York: Basic Books, 1972.

Hage, Jerold. *Communication and Organization Control: Cybernetics in Health and Welfare Settings.* New York: Wiley-Interscience, 1974.

Hall, Edward T. *The Hidden Dimension.* Garden City, N.Y.: Doubleday, 1966.

Henderson, A.M., and Parsons, Talcott, eds. *Max Weber: The Theory of Social and Economic Change.* New York: Oxford University Press, 1947.

Hickey, Thomas B., and Rypka, David J. "Automatic Detection of Duplicate Monographic Records." *Journal of Library Automation* 12 (June 1979):125–142.

Hoos, Ida R. *Systems Analysis in Public Policy.* Berkeley: University of California Press, 1972.

Johnson, Edward R., and Mann, Stuart H. *Organization Development for Academic Libraries: An Evaluation of the Management Review and Analysis Program.* Westport, Conn.: Greenwood Press, 1980.

Kaplan, Louis, "The Literature of Participation: From Optimism to Realism." *College and Research Libraries* 36 (1975):473–479.

King, Gerald W. *Automation and the Library of Congress.* Washington, D.C.: Library of Congress, 1963.

Lancaster, F. Wilfred. "The Future of Indexing and Abstracting Services." *Journal of American Society for Information Science* 33 (May 1982): 184.

Leinhardt, Samuel, ed. *Social Networks: A Developing Paradigm.* New York: Academic Press, 1977.

Lewin, Kurt; Lippitt, Ronald; and White, Ralph K. "Patterns of Aggressive Behavior in Experimentally Controlled Social 'Climates.'" *Journal of Social Psychology* 10 (1939):271–299.

Likert, Rensis. *New Patterns of Management.* New York: McGraw-Hill, 1961.

Lyden, Fremont J., and Miller, Ernest G., eds. *Planning, Programming, Budgeting.* Chicago: Markham Publishing, 1968.

Machine Readable Cataloging 1982–83, MARC Services, Cataloging Distribution Service. Washington, D.C.: Library of Congress, 1982.

Malinconico, S. Michael, and Fasana, Paul J. *The Future of the Catalog: The Library's Choices.* White Plains, N.Y.: Knowledge Industry Publications, 1979.

March, James G., ed. *Handbook of Organizations.* Chicago: Rand McNally, 1965.

Martin, Susan K. *Library Networks 1976–77.* White Plains, N.Y.: Knowledge Industry Publications, 1976.

Martin, Susan K. *Library Networks 1981–82.* White Plains, N.Y.: Knowledge Industry Publications, 1981.

Martyn, John, and Lancaster, F. Wilfred. *Investigative Methods in Library and Information Science.* Arlington, Va.: Information Resources Press, 1981.

Miller, Susan L. "The Evolution of an On-line Catalog." In *New Horizons for Academic Libraries,* edited by R.D. Stueart and R.D. Johnson. New York: K.G. Saur, 1979.

Moreno, J.L. "Experimental Sociometry and the Experimental Method in Science." In *Current Trends in Social Psychology,* edited by W. Dennis. Pittsburgh: University of Pittsburgh Press, 1948.

Moreno, J.L. *Who Shall Survive?* New York: Beacon House, 1953.

Nielen, G.C. "Foundations for a Curriculum in 'Large Systems.'" In *Education and Large Information Systems,* edited by R.G. Buckingham. Amsterdam: North Holland Publishing Company, 1977.

Overhage, Carl F.J., and Harman, R. Joyce, eds. *INTREX: Report of a Planning Commission on Information Transfer Experiments.* Cambridge, Mass.: MIT Press, 1965.

Parker, Edwin B. "Developing a Campus Information System." In *Collaborative Library Systems Development,* edited by P.J. Fasana and A. Veaner. Cambridge, Mass.: MIT Press, 1971.

Parsons, Talcott. *Structure and Process in Modern Societies.* New York: Morrow, 1980.

Rand Corporation Annual Report. Santa Monica: Rand Corporation, 1981.

Reeves, William. *Librarians as Professionals.* Lexington, Mass.: D.C. Heath and Co., Lexington Books, 1980.

Salmon, Stephen R. *Library Automation Systems.* New York: Marcel Dekker, Inc., 1975.

Sheehy, Eugene P. *Guide to Reference Books.* 9th ed. Chicago: American Library Association, 1976.

Shurkin, Joel. "The Rise and Fall and Rise of RLG." *American Libraries* 13 (1982):450–455.

Stogdill, Ralph M., ed. *Handbook of Leadership: Survey of Theory and Research.* New York: Free Press, 1974.

Summer, Robert, *Personal Space: A Behavioral Basis for Design.* Engle-
    wood Cliffs, N.J.: Prentice-Hall, 1969.
Taylor, Robert S. *The Making of the Library.* New York: Wiley-Becker-
    Hayes, 1972.
Toffler, Alvin. *Future Shock.* New York: Bantam Books, 1970.
Toffler, Alvin. *The Third Wave.* New York: Morrow, 1980.
Toohill, Barbara G. *Guide to Library Automation.* McLean, Va.: The
    Mitre Corporation, 1980.
Zeisel, John. *Sociology and Architectural Design.* New York: Russell Sage
    Foundation, 1975.

Index

AACR, 6–7, 84

Access: to bibliographies, 9; to files, 43; to other data bases, 69

Accountability, 170–171

Accounting, 133–134

Acquisitions: in branch libraries, 77–78; computer failure in, 76–77; defined, 3; methods of, 3–4; at Northwestern University, 53, 57; on-line search in, 78–79; on organizational chart, 10; organizational structure of, 75–79; responsibility for, 11; of serials, 85–88; in special collections, 78; at Stanford University, 49; steps in, 3; at University of Chicago, 32, 34–36; at University of Washington, 59. *See also* Collection management; Technical services

Action dates, 53

Adhocracy, 131

Administrative services: on organizational chart, 10; role in library policy, 9; at Stanford University, 44; at University of Chicago, 34

Advisory committee, 9, 10, 155

Allocation of budget: amounts, 28; for bibliographers, 81; process of, 133; at University of Chicago, 29

Anglo-American Cataloging Rules (AACR), 6–7, 84

Approval plans, 4

Authority: distribution of, 109–110; and information systems, 113; leadership and, 153–156; and supervisory structure, 71–72

Authority control, 83

Authority file, 82–83; and bibliographic records, 83

Authority structure, 6. *See also* Authority; Supervisory structure

Automation activities: batch systems for, 13; centralized vs. decentralized, 67, 125–127; history of, 13–19; initiation point of, 67; integration of, 65; National Science Foundation support of, 65–66; on-line search systems, 14; on organizational chart, 12; reasons for, 13; turnkey systems for, 14. *See also* Computer systems; Systems unit

BALLOTS, 16; adoption by RLG of, 42–43, 68–69; at Stanford University, 41–44. *See also* Research Libraries Information Network (RLIN)

Bar codes: system for, 92; at University of Chicago, 33

Batch systems, 13

Benefits, vs. costs, 139–145

Bibliographers: defined, 11; effect of budget cuts on, 81; at University of Chicago, 38

Bibliographic Automation of Large Library Operations Using a Timesharing System (BALLOTS), 16; adoption by RLG of, 42–43, 68–69; at Stanford University, 41–44. *See also* Research Libraries Information Network (RLIN)

Bibliographic control, 174

Bibliographic-data cooperatives: BALLOTS system, 16; browsability of files in, 17–18; catalog maintenance services of, 17; communication patterns within, 127–128; cost-benefit analysis of, 144–145; defined, 14–15; OCLC services, 15–19; other services of, 18; overlapping, 18; RLIN group, 16–18; WLN group, 17, 18

Bibliographic Item File (BIF), 32

Bibliographic Services Development Program, 129

Bibliographies: access to, 9; and authority files, 83; compilation of, 9; at Northwestern University,

About the Authors

Hugh F. Cline is a sociologist trained at the University of Stockholm and Harvard University. He has taught at the University of California, Santa Barbara, and Columbia University. Prior to joining the Research Division at Educational Testing Service, Dr. Cline served as a staff member and subsequently as president of Russell Sage Foundation.

Loraine T. Sinnott has had graduate training in both mathematics and the application of technology to social settings, receiving degrees from Stanford University and the University of Southern California. Prior to joining Educational Testing Service, Dr. Sinnott was on the staff of EDUCOM, the Interuniversity Communications Council, Inc.